LET'S SKATE

MINNESOTA!

LET'S SKATE MINNESOTA!

Where to Roll
Indoors and Outdoors

by Barbara J. Shotwell

and The Squarest Wheels

This book was designed and produced by Independence Press, Inc., Minneapolis, Minnesota.

Cartography by Independence Press, Inc.

Cover design and cartoon illustrations by Mike Christiansen.

Library of Congress card number 92-080788

ISBN 0-9632311-5-4

Disclaimer

All in-line skaters are urged to use good judgment in selecting their equipment and in choosing the places where they skate. The trails described here are subject to considerable change due to a variety of factors. In addition, since a skater's age, experience, and equipment will greatly affect personal safety, the authors can assume no responsibility for injuries resulting from the use of any trail selected from this guide.

Contents

Contents

About the Authors

The Squarest Wheels is a group of colorful south Minneapolis skaters known for their skating passion and audacious spirit. Its members are:

Dr. F

Joel *The Blade* **Fleischer**	Minneapolis financier and amateur geologist
Can Do **Andrew** **Magisano**	The Bead Master
Denise *Big D* **Pardello**	Trailblazing corporate consultant and Gloria Estefan impersonator
Truly **Julie** **Schmiel**	Downtown stockbroker and political operative

Their leader, **Barbara Jean Shotwell**, is a Minneapolis investment manager just back from skating the Panama Canal and still hoping to "Skate Tasmania" for CBS Sports.

Foreword

Back in the early 1980s I left the Winnipeg Jets hockey organization to develop the in-line roller skate. At that time, I thought of the skate as an off-season training tool for hockey players and skiers. It didn't take long for me to realize that in-line skates had tremendous potential as a general fitness and recreational item. Since then, in-line skating has become far more than the training tool and curiosity it was a decade ago. All across the country, the in-line skating trend has exploded – but nowhere has it reached the level of popularity it enjoys in Minnesota, my home state.

Skaters now outnumber bikers and runners on many of Minnesota's paved paths and trails, and the trend shows no signs of slowing down. The tremendous technological advances of the past decade have produced skates that are lighter, safer, and easier to use. The skate of the 1990s is comfortable, fast, and easy-to-maintain. Wrist guards, helmets, and other protective gear have also helped make skating safer, as have the numerous and well-maintained skating paths scattered throughout our state.

It's not surprising that Minnesota should have such a wonderful network of skating paths. The first practical in-line skate was developed here, and three of the major in-line skate manufacturers are located in the Twin Cities area. The quality of skates continues to improve, with innovations such as the original Rollerblade®, the SwitcH*it*® Interchangeable Skate System, and the new skating products now being created by O.S. Designs, my most recent venture. The in-line skate of the future will be even faster, lighter, and more comfortable. Better wheels, boots, and braking systems may make skating even more popular than bicycling. Perhaps the in-line skate will become the preferred mode of transport for the commuter of the future. Imagine thousands of men and women in business clothes, wrist guards, and helmets, all skating to and from work!

The demand for safe skating paths will continue to grow as the sport increases in popularity. The hundreds of miles of paths so wonderfully described in this book are there for you to use. Minnesota's outdoor skating paths are the finest in the nation, and during the winter the Metrodome in downtown Minneapolis offers some of the best indoor rolling around.

One final note – with the sudden increase in the number of new skaters, safety has become an increasingly important concern of mine. One of the best things a new skater can do is to start out slowly. Try getting used to your new skates by first wearing them

Foreword

on a carpet or a lawn, and then in a safe place with no traffic. Avoid streets, uneven sidewalks, and especially hills, until you know your limitations. It won't take long for you to get the feel of your skates. When you are comfortable, head for the nearest skating path and get ready to roll. Have a great time!

Scott Olson

Inventor of the original Rollerblade® and the SwitcH*it*® Interchangeable Skate System

Mr. Olson recently founded O.S. Designs, a product development group specializing in the in-line skate industry.

Let's Skate

Where to skate? We've found forty-five answers lying within the Twin Cities metropolitan area and throughout Minnesota. This book stemmed from our personal need for new skating adventures and has grown into a reference containing the information gathered from those experiences. In addition, we've added a few light touches of humor that we feel characterize the spirit and fun of this booming pastime, in-line skating.

All of the trails listed here were originally constructed as bike paths. There are, of course, many bike (and walking) trails that are unsuitable for in-line skating, and those have been excluded. In order to convey some measure of the suitability of each trail, we have constructed the following convention for its *difficulty*, based primarily on the terrain of the trail:

Beginner   the trail is generally flat and has no exceptionally dangerous curves or hills

Intermediate   the path includes some segments with curves, hills, surface conditions, or traffic that cannot be skated safely by an inexperienced skater

Advanced   the trail has steep hills and sharp curves that make it too difficult to be skated, under control, by any but the most experienced skaters

In a similar fashion, we have used the comparative terms *satisfactory, good,* and *excellent* to describe the general quality of the pavement of each trail. The paths labeled *satisfactory* are definitely skateable although they have a somewhat rough surface and high number of cracks. Paths characterized as *good* have smoother pavement and fewer cracks. Most *excellent* paths have been recently resurfaced and contain no significant sections with less than superior quality.

Most of the trails in this guide allow two-way skating and biking. The few exceptions are noted as one-way in the *surface* descriptions.

Let's Skate

The following symbols are used on the maps:

ⓟ Parking

ⓘ Information

⚠ Caution

├--┤ Caution zone

At many of these trail sites, there is a fee for parking. It turns out that the rates charged by county and state parks are the same: $18 annual fee or $4/day per car.

If you have a county pass from one county, it is honored by all other county parks. Similarly, any state park's annual pass will get you free parking at all other state parks.

The map we have included with each trail description is meant to serve three purposes: to help you get there, to show you the skating route, and to locate some areas where caution is advised. Detailed maps of each trail are generally available on-site at no charge. You may also obtain a map through the mail by calling the friendly parks people whose phone number is listed on the trail description.

See you on the trail!

Safety

Wearing the proper equipment will not only reduce your risk of injury but also make your skating experiences more enjoyable.

Equipment

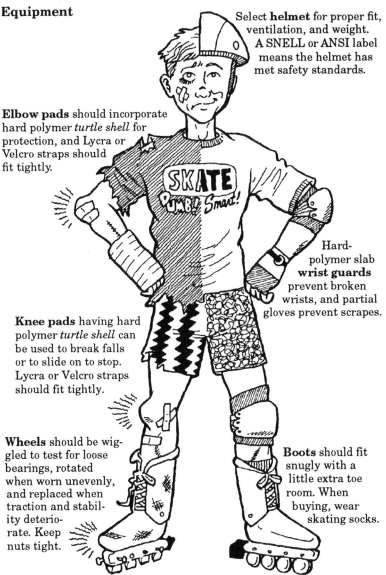

Select **helmet** for proper fit, ventilation, and weight. A SNELL or ANSI label means the helmet has met safety standards.

Elbow pads should incorporate hard polymer *turtle shell* for protection, and Lycra or Velcro straps should fit tightly.

Hard-polymer slab **wrist guards** prevent broken wrists, and partial gloves prevent scrapes.

Knee pads having hard polymer *turtle shell* can be used to break falls or to slide on to stop. Lycra or Velcro straps should fit tightly.

Wheels should be wiggled to test for loose bearings, rotated when worn unevenly, and replaced when traction and stability deteriorate. Keep nuts tight.

Boots should fit snugly with a little extra toe room. When buying, wear skating socks.

Brakes should be replaced when angle with road is 45° or more.

3

Stopping

There are five general techniques for stopping:

1. Apply the heel brake by extending forward the leg that has the brake, raising the toes up, and exerting pressure on the road with the brake pad.

2. Use the T-stop by raising one skate behind the other, turning it perpendicular to the skating direction, and dragging the inner edge of the wheels on the road surface.

3. Employ a controlled 360° turn by slowing down with your feet turned out.

4. For advanced skaters only, resort to the power stop by abruptly turning the forward skate perpendicular to the skating direction and bringing the rear skate ahead with the rollers perpendicular to your motion as you lean back.

5. Bail out by heading off the path onto grass or a soft surface.

IISA™ Rules of the Road

The International In-line Skating Association, discussed in the next chapter, has developed the following advice for skaters:

1. Wear protective gear including a helmet, knee and elbow pads, and wrist guards.

2. Achieve a basic skating level before taking to the road.

3. Stay alert and be courteous at all times.

4. Always skate under control.

5. Skate on the right side of paths, trails, and sidewalks.

6. Overtake pedestrians, cyclists, and other skaters on the left.

7. Stay away from water, oil, or debris on the trail, and uneven or broken pavement.

8. Observe all traffic regulations.

9. Avoid areas with heavy automobile traffic.

10. Always yield to pedestrians.

In-Line Info

History

Strictly speaking, the in-line skate is a very old device, dating back to 18th century Holland where an enterprising ice skater used wooden spools and strips of wood to convert his shoes into summertime skates. After side-by-side roller skates were introduced in 1863, there were only sporadic attempts to develop an in-line skate over the next 100 years. In the 1980s, Scott Olson founded Rollerblade, Inc., which refined the design and expanded the market for in-line skating by promoting it as a new sport.

The modern materials and technology incorporated in today's skates are considerably more advanced than the original wooden spools. At first, steel was used to form the skate frame needed to withstand high stress and provide impact resistance. Now, space-age plastics can provide the same strength with less weight. In addition, it is possible to mold the plastic in more complex shapes so that many of the additional bolts and fasteners needed with steel can be eliminated by designing their function into the frame. These modern skates thus ride more smoothly and quietly than the metal versions, are more resistant to abrasion and chemical deterioration, and provide more freedom in choosing bright colors.

Fitness

Rollerblade, Inc. commissioned Dr. Carl Foster, Coordinator of Sports Medicine and Sports Science for the United States Speed Skating Team, to conduct a study of the fitness effects of in-line skating. Here is a summary of the results of that study regarding expended calories and aerobic benefits.

Calories

Thirty minutes of steady, recreational in-line skating produces a heart rate of about 148 beats per minute and burns about 285 calories. Speed skating for thirty minutes can burn about 450 calories. These rates bracket those for running (350 calories minute) and bicycling (360 calories per minute) and are in the range of the 300 calories per minute workout recommended by the American College of Sports Medicine.

Aerobics

The aerobic benefits, that is, the improvements in the body's ability to supply oxygen to the heart, are greater than from cycling but not as great as from running, principally because a runner cannot coast. Skating, however, is better than either cycling or running at strengthening stomach, thigh, and hip muscles and produces less impact on hip, knee, ankle, and foot joints than running does.

Cross Training

There are several sports for which in-line skating can serve as an excellent complementary regimen because it provides essential conditioning or skills. Hockey players are the traditional beneficiaries of off-season in-line skating but speedskaters, figure skaters, downhill and cross-country skiers, bicyclists, and runners are also finding that in-lining gives them an efficient means for increasing their competitive edge.

Competition

Racing

Racing is becoming an increasingly organized and widespread activity. Most races are 10 kilometers in length but there are also shorter sprint events of 200 to 500 meters as well as longer races of 50 to 100 kilometers throughout the United States.

In 1988 Karen Edwards, a Minneapolis attorney, shocked the roller skating world by placing first in Georgia's Athens-to-Atlanta race, two hours ahead of the second place woman! Since then, outdoor speed skating has been dominated by the in-line skate.

Although there are technical debates about why five wheels are better for racing than four, it seems that the advantage is actually gained from the extra length of the frame, which produces a longer, more stable stride.

More exotic races such as relays and even a biathlon involving skating and archery are starting to appear throughout the nation.

Rollerhockey

Rollerhockey is a non-contact game of two five-member teams playing under rules similar to ice hockey. The object of play is to put the puck in the opponen'ts goal. Each team consists of a goaltender, two defenders, and two forwards. Since there is one fewer forward than in ice hockey, and since there is no offside rule, the action is more wide-open with more breakaways across the 180-by-85-foot rink.

Almost every major city in the nation has at least one rollerhockey league. The grand plan is to eventually attain status as an Olympic event. Call the International In-line Skating Association (800-FOR-IISA) for information about league activities and tournaments.

Tips

Here are a few simple pointers that can enhance your skating experience.

Preparing for the road

If you are inexperienced, get the feel of your skates on indoor carpeting or grass first.

Practice in a controlled environment such as a parking lot or indoor skating rink to gain minimal competency.

Test your equipment. Wiggle the wheels to make sure they are tight on the axles and the bearings are not worn excessively. Make sure the nuts are tight. Double check that the brake is not worn down excessively.

Packing for the road

Wear a small fanny pack with some of the following items: water bottle; light-weight sandals; candy, chocolate, or nuts for energy; extra pair of socks; skate wrenches; blister treatment kit.

LifeSavers, SweetTarts, and GatorGum are good choices for mouth moisteners that may be needed to counteract that dry feeling a long skate often produces.

During a long skate, it may be necessary to change to a dry pair of socks in order to avoid blistering.

Putting New-Skin on a developing blister can prevent its progress.

On the road

Do not wear radio headsets on busy trails because you may not hear traffic approaching from the rear.

For increased vision, attach a rear view mirror to the wrist guard with Velcro.

Slower skaters keep to the right.

Shout, "On your left," when passing.

Start speed control at the *top* of a hill, not after building up speed on the way down.

In-Line Info

Downhill slopes should be traversed in a zig-zag fashion to limit speed.

Use ski poles to provide additional stability.

A hockey stick (preferably with plastic tip) can also help with balance and speed reduction by dragging it behind.

It is often too late if you wait until you are thirsty to drink fluids. On a hot humid day, it is essential to take in liquids regularly.

Wear two pairs of socks to reduce the occurrence of blisters. A thin liner sock will absorb moisture and a lightweight wool sock over it provides comfortable padding.

Use your water bottle to spray menacing dogs.

International In-line Skating Association (IISA™)

The world of in-line skating has a leadership organization whose primary purpose is to service the recreational, competitive, and safety needs of in-line skaters throughout the United States and internationally. The International In-line Skating Association (IISA™) was formed in July 1991 by seven Charter Members representing the following name brands:

Bauer®

CCM®

Kryptonics®

Roller Derby®

Rollerblade®

Ultra Wheels®

Variflex®

The IISA™ is constructed to be an independent organization, not dominated by any single manufacturer or special interest, but rather devoted solely to the growth of in-line skating as a whole. Its objectives are to:

- Promote the safe and courteous use of in-line skates

- Protect and expand access for in-line skaters to streets, sidewalks, roads, highways, trails, and other public places

- Develop the IISA™ Competition Committee as the international governing body of in-line skating

- Provide IISA™ members with excellent customer service

Examples of the IISA™'s activities include the defeat of skating bans in Ann Arbor, Michigan; Monterey, California; Orlando, Florida; Birmingham, Michigan; Poolesville, Maryland; and Newport Beach, California, as well as sanctioning and providing officials for a 50K New York City racing championship and a 10K race in Los Angeles.

The project that the organization is most enthusiastic about is its SkateSmart™ safety campaign, which seeks to help newcomers to the sport get started using their skates properly and safely. The in-line manufacturers associated with this national drive have distributed more than four million safety posters, fliers, and hangtags to retailers and consumers. In addition, they have established ten *Rules of the Road* (*see* page 4) incorporating a few common sense guidelines about respecting the rights of outdoor enthusiasts.

The headquarters of the IISA™ is located right here in Minnesota at 3033 Excelsior Boulevard, Minneapolis, MN 55416. You can obtain information about the organization or membership by calling either (612) 924-2348 or 1-800-FOR-IISA. Membership benefits include a newsletter and event fee reductions.

Metro Trail Listing

Minneapolis

Central
31. Minneapolis Central
32. Minneapolis East
33. Minneapolis West

North
3. Anoka County Riverfront Park
8. Bunker Hills Regional Park
17. Elm Creek Park Reserve
36. North Hennepin Trail Corridor
39. Rice Creek West Regional Trail
41. Sand Creek / Coon Creek Trail
42. Shingle Creek Trailway / Palmer Lake

South
6. Bloomington City Trails
7. Bredesen Park
9. Bush Lake Park
13. Cleary Lake Regional Park
19. Fort Snelling State Park
25. Hyland Lake Park Reserve
27. Lake Cornelia
34. Minnesota Valley State Trail
35. Normandale Lake
37. Opus Loop Trail System

West
4. Baker Park Reserve
12. Carver Park Reserve
18. Fish Lake Regional Park
20. French Regional Park
28. Lake Rebecca Park Reserve

Saint Paul

Central
5. Battle Creek Regional Park
14. Como Park
21. Gateway Segment of Willard Munger State Trail
38. Phalen-Keller Regional Park

East
1. Afton City Trail
2. Afton State Park

North
29. Long Lake Regional Park

South
23. Hidden Falls / Crosby Farm
30. Mendota Heights Trail

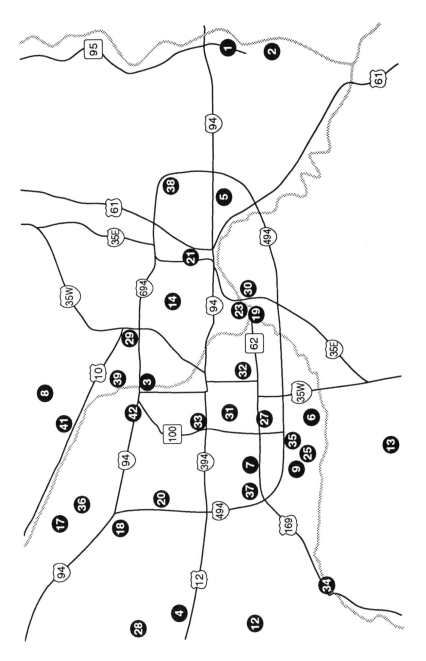

Greater Minnesota Trail Listing

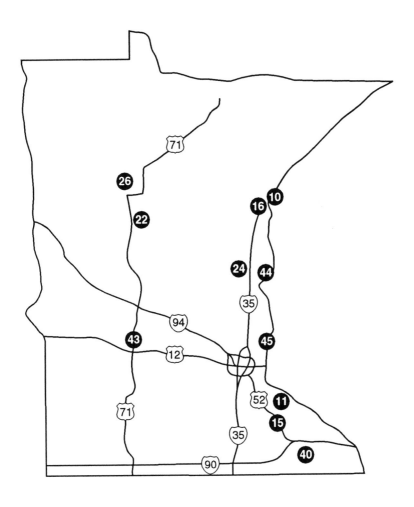

1 Afton City Trail
Almost a (Wiscon) Sin

This is an excellent 3.5 mile path for a modest workout. It is lightly used, and situated in an extremely attractive and popular part of the state.

Where   Afton, Minnesota, twenty miles east of St. Paul

Length   3.5 miles

Difficulty   *Beginner.* Flat, comparatively straight, lightly used trail.

Surface   Good

Terrain   Follows alongside State Highway 95. There are only a couple of very modest hills as the trail makes a few welcome turns into the woods.

Facilities

Parking   In park-and-ride lot at the junction of the frontage road and Interstate 94. At the southern end, parking is available on-street in Afton.

Food   About halfway through the trail is a small roadhouse called the Valley Trail Cafe that serves burgers and fries.

Markers   Less than a mile from Afton is a marker commemorating one of the earliest flour mills in Minnesota – the Bolles Flour Mill on Bolles Creek.

Nearby   The charming town of Afton provides access to the St. Croix River as well as to Afton State Park, which has superior park, swimming, and camping facilities, as well as hiking and biking trails.

The Afton House offers excellent dining, and its more casual part, the Catfish Saloon, is great for a sandwich and a beer. Luerck's is famous for its Luercksburgers. If the place had a telephone, you could use it to locate a restroom.

For skaters who would rather dine alfresco, there is a deli/grocery store across the street from the Afton House.

Phone   Afton City Hall   (612) 436-5090

Get There Go east on Interstate 94 to just before the Wisconsin line, then south on State Highway 95 to Afton. The trail starts near the Afton City Hall and goes north to the frontage road of 94.

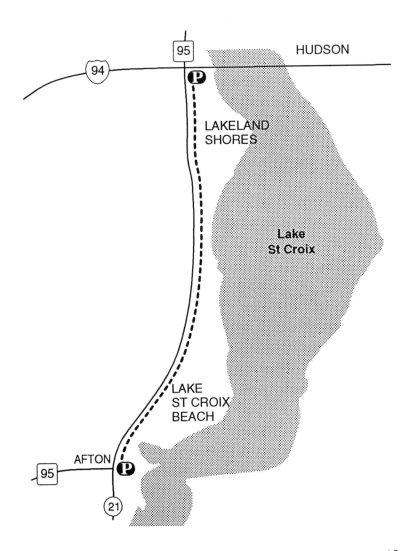

2 Afton State Park
On Your Aft

The extraordinary scenery along this trail can probably be enjoyed by only the most advanced skaters because of its steep hills and sharp curves. You may happen by Karen Edwards, the national women's racing champion, or Ron Lowrie, one of the top five competitors in national men's racing, both of whom train in the area – let us know if you pass them up!

Where In Afton State Park, about four miles south of the city of Afton

Length 2 miles

Difficulty *Advanced.* Steep hills.

Surface Good

Terrain Beautiful St. Croix Valley scenery with hills and bluffs overlooking meadows and woodlands

Facilities

Parking Very ample at several lots in the park

Restrooms At park headquarters and throughout the park

Picnic Sites Grills, tables, and benches at several designated sites

Other Excellent swimming beach and hiking trails

Nearby *See* the section describing the Afton City Trail (trail 1), which is about four miles to the north on State Highway 21.

Phone Afton State Park Manager   (612) 436-5391

Get There Go east on Interstate 94 to just before the Wisconsin line, then south on State Highway 95 to Afton. Continue straight south on State Highway 21 about four miles to the park entrance on your left.

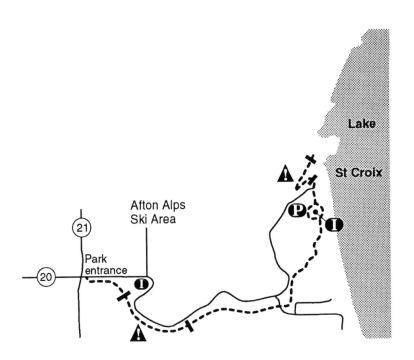

⚠ **Caution** There is a downhill slope near the west end of the trail that is frequently covered with gravel and sand. Also there is a downhill grade with a sharp curve at the north end of the trail.

3 Anoka County Riverfront Park
A Double Bump

A short, scenic trail whose two hills provide a good workout

Where Fridley, seven miles north of Minneapolis

Length 1.75 miles

Difficulty *Intermediate.* Two substantial hills.

Surface Good

Terrain The trail follows alongside the Mississippi River over gently rolling hills and through open meadows with a couple of wooded areas providing some welcome shade.

Facilities

Parking The largest lot is at the north end; smaller lots are at the south end and in front of the children's playground.

Restrooms At both shelters, located north and south of the Ridell Mansion

Picnic Sites Throughout the park and at the two shelters, where there are grills and running water

Other Playground area and exercise course. The Ridell Mansion is open to the public and available by reservation for meetings or group social events.

Phone Anoka County Parks   (612) 757-3920

Get There Take Interstate 694 to one mile east of State Highway 100, exiting on East River Road. Proceed south one-half mile on East River Road to the park entrance on your right. At the tee, turn right and follow the road to the parking lot on your left.

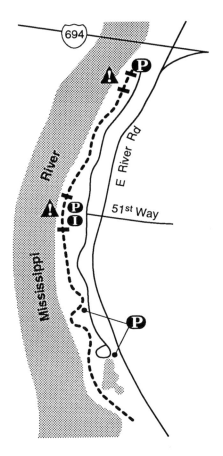

⚠ **Caution** The steep slope as you leave the north parking lot may cause some to prefer walking to the top of the hill before skating. Returning over this downhill slope can be even more challenging. There is also a substantial hill midway on the trail behind the Ridell Mansion (big, white house).

4 Baker Park Reserve
Swan Song

If the hills are filled with the sound of music, it is more likely to be due to the trumpeting swan population than to Al Hirt.

Where Approximately twenty miles west of Minneapolis between Orono and Maple Plain

Length 6.2 miles

Difficulty *Intermediate.* Many rolling hills.

Surface Excellent. Smooth with few cracks.

Terrain Hilly with gradual turns. Most of the trail length is sunny meadowland but there are stretches of woods.

Facilities

Parking Ample at park entrance

Restrooms Permanent at park entrance; one portable midway

Picnic Sites Several scattered along the trail; only one with water and only one other with restrooms

Camping One small off-road site

Nearby Baker Park Reserve is noted for its trumpeter swan refuge, and many people might have an interest in seeing these magnificent birds. The refuge is down a dirt road so it is useful to bring walking shoes as well as binoculars.

The Keg N Cork is a small, boisterous bar with reasonable prices standing just one-half mile from the trailhead, at the junction of U.S. Highway 12 and County Road 24. Hamburger baskets appear to be the culinary mainstay.

Several miles east of the trailhead is Orono's Red Rooster, a bar and restaurant specializing in hamburgers.

Billy's Lighthouse on Long Lake is owned by the same people as T Wright's. It has excellent standard fare: hamburgers, Reubens, barbecued ribs, steaks, and fish or shrimp baskets, as well as full bar service. For casual dining, it features an outdoor deck overlooking Long Lake.

Phone   Entrance gate   (612) 479-2258
            Campground reservations
              and office   (612) 476-4666

Get There   Take U.S. Highway 12 past Orono to County Road 29 and go north about one-half mile to the park entrance on the right.

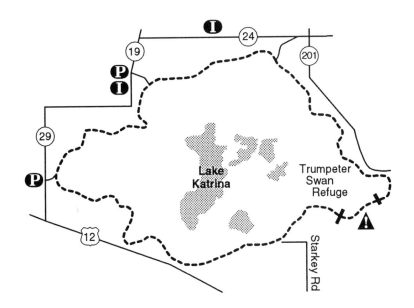

⚠️**Caution**   Several of the hills are moderately steep but there are no sharp curves at the bottoms.

5 Battle Creek Regional Park
No Battle Here

This park offers fairly typical skating fare and is extremely popular with neighboring 3Mers.

Where　　　Maplewood, east of McKnight Road

Length　　　3.85 miles

Difficulty　*Beginner.* Flat without sharp curves.

Surface　　Good. One-way skating.

Terrain　　Wooded, rolling hills

Facilities

Parking　Free parking at the park entrance

Restrooms　At the picnic pavilion

Picnic Site　The picnic pavilion is open to family-sized parties without reservations and has kitchen facilities to accommodate reservations for groups up to five hundred. It is heavily booked, often months in advance.

Nearby　　3M employees will enjoy the skyline view of their corporate headquarters.

Phone　　Ramsey County Parks
and Recreation　　　　(612) 777-1707

Get There　From the Twin Cities, go east on Interstate 94 to McKnight Road. Go south on McKnight Road for 0.6 miles to Upper Afton Road and turn left (east) to the park entrance, which is one block on the left.

Battle Creek Regional Park

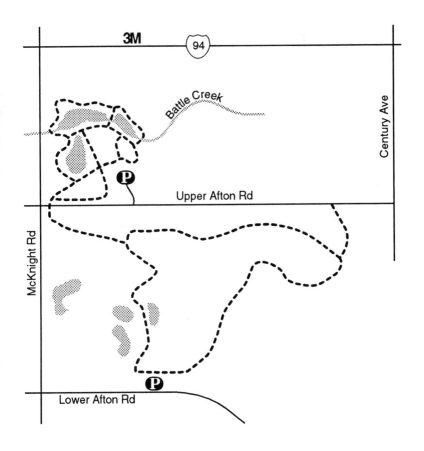

6 Bloomington City Trails
Roll Your Own

Sometimes the most overlooked facilities for skaters are in their own backyards. Prestigious West Bloomington provides a unique assortment of honeycombed trails that can be combined in many ways for a personalized skating experience. Future plans call for connecting with the systems of neighboring communities.

Where   Bloomington

Length   This trail can be worked to provide a skate of virtually any length. The run from the intersection of Bloomington Ferry Road and Old County Road 18 to the shopping center near Old Shakopee Road and Interstate 35W is approximately 7 miles.

Difficulty   *Intermediate.* Several busy intersections. Except for the region marked on the map, the main route is flat. Some of the side-trips include formidable hills.

Surface   Varies between good and excellent

Terrain   For the most part these routes are flat; however, there are sharp hills in the area.

Nearby   The main route begins in a small strip mall at the junction of Old County Road 18 and Bloomington Ferry Road on the Bloomington-Eden Prairie border. One of the advantages of urban skating is the convenience of being able to buy liquids along the way, making it unnecessary to carry water. For example, the shopping area contains a Super America and a Tom Thumb for liquids, as well as a reasonable Chinese restaurant, the Lai Inn, for lunch.

The route proceeds south and east on Bloomington Ferry Road until its intersection with Old Shakopee Road where Dred Scott Field offers softball diamonds and tennis courts. For a small fee, you can also test your swing against 70 MPH baseballs or arching softballs from a bevy of batting machines.

The trail continues two miles east along Old Shakopee Road past Normandale Boulevard to France

Avenue where you might enjoy any of several small restaurants for lunch: the Taiwan Restaurant in the Valley West Shopping Center, as well as the Don Ho and Andy's Tap, noted for burgers, across the street in a little strip mall on Old Shakopee Road. There is also a McDonald's in the Valley West Shopping Center lot. For the skater in need of repairs or equipment, Penn Cycle has a store in the shopping center.

Going farther east on Old Shakopee Road you pass Cal's Market, one of the more complete farmers' markets in the Twin Cities area and an excellent source of fresh fruits and vegetables in season.

A couple of miles farther east, the road curves south to its terminating junction with Interstate 35W where there are a several shops including REI, an excellent source for outdoor and skating gear; Burger Brothers; and Byerly's.

Side Trips One of the beauties of skating Bloomington is the wide range of possible side trips.

Trip 1 After leaving the shopping center at Bloomington Ferry Road and Old County Road 18, head east on Veness Road, up a small hill and down another, to a junction with West Bush Lake Road. Head south for about one-third mile on this bucolic, almost country road, until you see the entrance to a bike path on the left. No motorized vehicles are permitted. This path leads into Bush Lake Park, where you can take advantage of the quiet trails there (trail 9).

Trip 1A Instead of heading south on West Bush Lake Road, take the bike path north to West 86th Street where you can cross East Bush Lake Road and then head south to enter Hyland Park, with its excellent 5.75 mile trail system (trail 25).

Trip 1B Continue north on the bike path, past West 86th Street, past Telegraph Road, and on to Marth Road where there is a lovely bike path winding through some of the most serene terrain in Bloomington. After an easy mile's downhill skate, the path intersects with East Bush Lake Road. Located a few hundred yards east is the 2.25 mile, easy-rolling trail system of Normandale Lake (trail 35).

Trip 2   If you continue down Old Shakopee Road past Bush Lake Road and go north on Nesbitt Avenue, West 94th Street will take you into the Hyland Park trail system (trail 25).

Trip 3   Normandale Road can be taken north from Old Shakopee Road but the hills are rather steep, so this segment should be used by experts only.

Trip 4   You can go north on France Avenue but this route is also only for the expert.

Trip 5   *The Eden Prairie Adventure.* Go west on Anderson Lakes Parkway instead of east on Bloomington Ferry Road. There is a lovely bike path through the preserve that can be taken all the way to U.S. Highway 169 in the west where Prairie Cycle can attend to any equipment needs that may have arisen, or north to the area around Eden Prairie Center, where you can enjoy the following facilities: Applebee's, Ciatti's, The Green Mill, and Chi Chi's, as well as a number of smaller restaurants. Liquids may be purchased at several fast food stores or gas stations.

Phone   Bloomington Parks and Recreation   (612) 887-9601

Get There   Take Interstate 494 and go south at exit number 10 (169 North). Proceed 1.5 miles south on Old County Road 18 to Bloomington Ferry Road, then turn left and make the first right into the small strip mall.

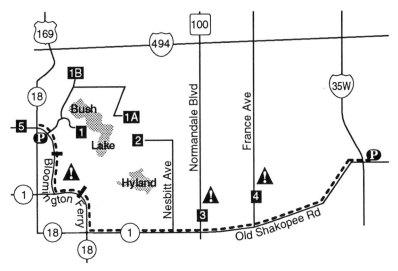

⚠ **Caution** There is a long gradual hill on Bloomington Ferry Road. The hills north of Old Shakopee Road on both Normandale Boulevard and France Avenue are for advanced skaters only. Several busy intersections along the trail need to be crossed.

7 Bredesen Park
Residential Rolling

A nice path to use for a quick workout but not suitable for a whole day affair due to the lack of facilities.

Where	Edina, off Vernon Avenue
Length	2.1 miles
Difficulty	*Intermediate*. Modest hills and curves.
Surface	Excellent. Separate paths for skating/biking and walking. The skating path was recently paved.
Terrain	The path's many hills and curves run through both woods and marshland.
Facilities	
Parking	Along Olinger Boulevard and also in the lot at the beginning of the trail
Restrooms	Only at the beginning of the path
Food	None
Picnic Site	None
Nearby	This trail is located in the middle of a residential area and is used mostly by local residents. There is a nature area along the path, accessible only by walking. Cold drinks can be obtained from a gas station about one-half mile down Vernon Avenue.
Phone	Edina Parks and Recreation (612) 927-8861
Get There	Take State Highway 62 to Gleason Road. Go north for three blocks on Gleason (which becomes Vernon Avenue) and turn right onto Olinger Boulevard. Continue about three blocks and make a right turn onto Olinger Road, which runs into the parking lot.

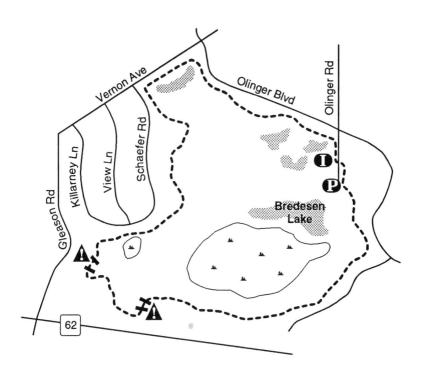

⚠**Caution** The two wooden bridges are approached going down-hill.

8 Bunker Hills Regional Park
An-o-kay Trail

This is an excellent spot to spend a day or a whole weekend, with lots to do for the entire family. The Animal Humane Society is on State Highway 14 in case you'd like to pick up a pet on the way home.

Where   Anoka County, on Andover–Coon Rapids border

Length   5.3 miles

Difficulty   *Beginner.* No steep hills or sharp curves.

Surface   Excellent

Terrain   Very flat. Surrounded by pines and low brush.

Facilities

Parking   Ample at various park locations. $2 if you don't have a county pass.

Restrooms   Available at the activity center and along the path

Picnic Sites   Nine shelters with tables and grills

Camping   26 sites, no electrical hookups

Other   Indoor and outdoor archery ranges

The activity center is available for group meetings but has no food.

Hay and sleigh rides. Trail rides every hour. Pony rides every half hour.

Phone

Activity center	(612) 757-3920
Camping reservations	(612) 757-3920
Golf	(612) 755-4140
Stables	(612) 757-7010
Wave pool	(612) 755-3672

Get There   Take Interstate 694 to State Highway 65 and go north about seven miles to State Highway 242 (Main Street). Proceed west on 242 for 2.5 miles and turn right, into the park. Brown sign one-half block inside gives directions to various activities.

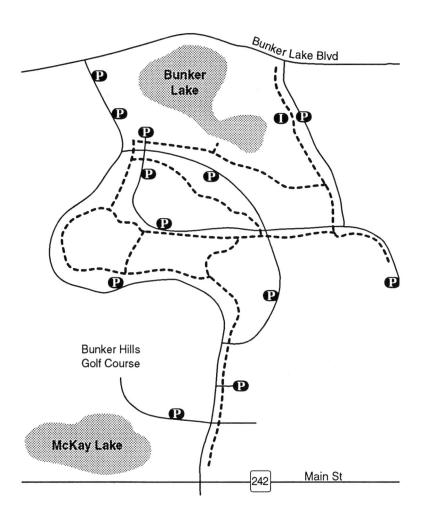

⚠ Caution Because the path veers off in many directions, pay close attention to your location. It is especially important to be aware of the many crossing roads that break up the path; these could be dangerous intersections if you lose control.

9 Bush Lake Park
A Bird In The Hand

A short trail in a lightly used park with excellent facilities. Probably best enjoyed as part of a longer trip (see Bloomington, trail 6) or as a Sunday family picnic in which skating will play only a partial role.

Where   Bloomington, between East and West Bush Lake Roads, south of Interstate 494

Length   1.5 miles

Difficulty   *Beginner.* Mostly level to very gently rolling. The northernmost section is a steady, gentle incline.

Surface   Excellent

Terrain   The first part of the trail involves a gentle, wooded, uphill grade along the shore of Bush Lake. The path is far enough from the lake to obscure its view along most of the trail. After about one-half mile, the trail emerges from the woods along the picnic and parking area, and continues south along the west shore of the lake, ending at West Bush Lake Road.

Facilities

Parking   Ample parking. $4/car per day.

Picnic Site   There is an excellent picnic area that is mostly shaded. Also a large grassy area can be used for a variety of lawn sports.

Children   The picnic area contains a playground which, while adequate, lacks the amazing scope of that at nearby Hyland Park.

Nearby   There are many other facilities at Bush Lake such as a boat launch, a swimming beach, a bath house, and volley ball and horseshoe areas. However, these are located at the picnic area on the east side of Bush Lake and are therefore better used in conjunction with Hyland Park since they can be reached from here only by skating over 1.5 miles of poor surface, open road on East Bush Lake Road.

Phone   Bloomington Parks and Recreation   (612) 887-9601

Get There Take Interstate 494 to Bush Lake Road. Go south about 1.5 miles. Entrance is on the left, off West 94th Street.

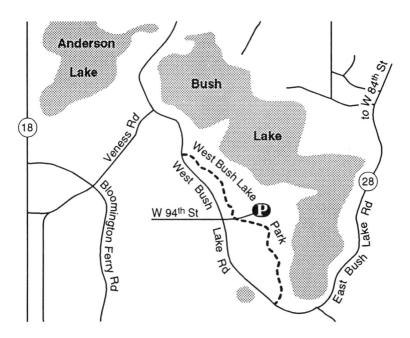

10 Canal Park
Short and Superior

An action-packed trail providing museums, the beauty of Lake Superior, and all the amenities of a tourist spot.

Where   Duluth, 150 miles north of Minneapolis, running between Fitger's Brewing Complex and Grandma's Saloon and Deli

Length   1.5 miles

Difficulty   *Beginner.* Straight and flat.

Surface   Good

Terrain   Flat trail running along the shore of Lake Superior

Facilities

Parking   Available everywhere along the trail and at both ends. There could be a charge, depending on where you park.

Restrooms   At Canal Park Marine Museum and any of the local restaurants or stores in the area

Food   Fast food available at Burger King or Hardee's. Visit the infamous Grandma's including its sports bar, which has indoor and outdoor basketball courts, volleyball and bocce ball (the Italian game of Guts and Glory) courts, and all the favorite video and bar games. Vendors along the trail sell everything from popcorn to ice cream. You can also visit Fitger's Brewing Complex for fast food or higher-priced menus.

Nearby   The city of Duluth provides all types of lodging ranging from the Downtown Radisson to camping. Fitger's Inn is an old brewery-turned-hotel offering quaint rooms and spectacular views of Lake Superior with ships passing in the night. Avoid the rooms above the bar.

Fitger's Brewing Complex and the DeWitt Seitz Building have antique and craft shops. There is also a casino with pull tabs, bingo, slots, and gaming tables at the Fond-Du-Luth. The park offers boat and horse carriage rides.

The Marine Museum and the Depot Museum are both worth visiting. You can spend hours touring the W. A. Irvin, a ship permanently moored in Superior Bay.

The famous Aerial Lift Bridge creates fifty-five seconds of pure excitement while ascending and another fifty-five as it returns.

Phone   Duluth Convention
              and Visitors Bureau   (218) 722-4011
              Fitger's Inn   (218) 722-8826 or 1-800-726-2982

Get There   From the Twin Cities take Interstate 35 north; exit on Superior Street in Duluth. Continue about a mile and turn right onto Lake Avenue. Follow the Canal Park signs.

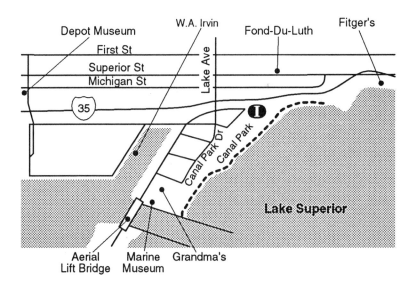

⚠ Caution Heavily-used trail

11 Cannon Valley Trail
Have A Cannon Ball

The middle section of this trail is scheduled to be paved during summer 1992. The beautiful scenery is no doubt a principal reason that the trail is so heavily used on weekends. Cannon Falls and Red Wing have a lot you can enjoy.

Where   60 miles southeast of the Twin Cities

Length   20.2 miles, the middle 7.7 miles of which is scheduled to be paved summer 1992. The Cannon Falls section is 6.8 miles long; the Red Wing leg is 5.2 miles. There is a half-mile extension to Anderson Park on the east end of the trail.

Difficulty   *Intermediate.* Several wooden bridges and road crossings.

Surface   Excellent

Terrain   Fairly flat trail with a slight upgrade heading away from Red Wing. The trail follows along the curves of the river, through wooded areas and by beautiful rock formations, every now and then passing fields with grazing cattle. Pretty well shaded by trees.

Facilities   Wheel pass is required. Five self-purchase stations are available along the trail. $2 daily; $7 annual; age eighteen and under, free.

Parking   Ample parking available at both ends of the trail and at Welch Station.

Restrooms   At each access point and along the trail. Water fountain at each restroom.

Food   When the trail is completed, its midpoint will be a short walk from the village of Welch where there is food.

Picnic Sites   At Anderson Memorial Rest Area, which is 1.5 miles west of Red Wing, and another located 3.5 miles east of Cannon Falls. Resting benches are placed all along the trail.

Nearby   There is lodging at the historic St. James Hotel in Red Wing. About twenty-five miles east of Red Wing, in Stockholm, Wisconsin, is the Merchants Hotel.

While there, you may to want to dine at The Harbor View in Pepin, which offers excellent meals and a romantic atmosphere. They do not take reservations but the wait is worthwhile.

CANNON FALLS One block off the beginning of the trail is Lorentz Meats serving deli sandwiches with outdoor seating. Downtown has the Pizza Barn and Brewster's Bar & Grill.

RED WING Godfather's Pizza, vendors, and small eateries are near The Pottery Barn, which is a conglomerate of name-brand factory outlet discount stores. The area also offers a flea market and many antique shops. Treasure Island Casino is located just outside of Red Wing off U.S. Highway 61.

Phone

Cannon Valley Trail (507) 263-3954

Red Wing Chamber of Commerce (612) 388-4719
420 Levee Street
Red Wing MN 55066

Cannon Falls Chamber of Commerce (507) 263-2289
103 4th Street North
Cannon Falls MN 55009

Merchants Hotel (715) 442-2113
Ask for Lucy, the proprietor.

St. James Hotel (612) 388-2846

Get There   *Cannon Falls access.* Take U.S. Highway 52 south to Cannon Falls; exit east onto State Highway 19 through the town of Cannon Falls and across a bridge to Bridge Street. Turn left; follow to East Stoughton Street and turn right; go four blocks. Parking is available across from the ball field.

Red Wing access. Take U.S. Highway 61 south to Red Wing; exit on Bench Street. Follow the trail signs about three blocks to parking.

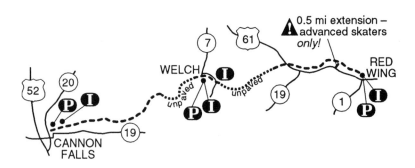

▲Caution   Trail due to be completed summer 1992. The path is well maintained but there are many wooden bridges and road crossings that require careful traversing

Trouble with your laces again?
That does it – you're going to Tieland!

12 Carver Park Reserve
A Best-Kept Secret

Very lightly used – truly a secret path. Since there are nearby hiking and horse trails, the biking/skating path has few walkers. Two special areas are Champion Point, overlooking Parley Lake, and the scenic overlook, which affords a beautiful view of the Fred E. King Waterbird Sanctuary on Parley Lake. The Lowry Nature Center has fascinating educational exhibits for both children and adults.

Where	In Victoria, approximately twenty miles southwest of Minneapolis
Length	7.85 miles
Difficulty	*Intermediate.* Modest hills, some rough pavement.
Surface	Good. Marbled blacktop. The skating quality of the part of the trail that was resurfaced in 1989 is not as good as that of the prior surface, some parts of which still remain.
Terrain	For the most part, gradual hills and curves. Speed can be controlled because downhills are followed by flat to moderate uphill terrain. Trail weaves through woods and meadows, and by several lakes.

Facilities

Parking	Ample at Lowry Nature Center and also at east end of trail, north of Highway 5
Restrooms	Lowry Nature Center, west end picnic area, Lake Auburn campground, junction of trail and road leading to picnic area
Food	None in Park Reserve. Water and pop machine in Lowry Nature Center.
Camping	Campground along beach area of Lake Auburn, fifty-four sites, no electrical hookups, $6.50/night. Children's play area. Ice available.
Picnic Site	West end of preserve, tables, shelter, volleyball net, softball diamond
Fishing	Boat launches on Stieger Lake, Lake Auburn, Lake Zumbra, and Parley Lake

Markers   On the trail northwest of Stieger Lake there is a plaque commemorating a section of track laid in 1886 as part of James Hill's Great Northern Railroad connecting Hopkins and Hutchinson until 1901. The trail passes over old railroad bed.

Nearby   Victoria has Food Mart on the east side and Dairy Queen on the west, both on State Highway 5. Leo's Bar is a great local hangout with snacks only, pool table. Schmidty's Bar has big screen TV, pool table, foosball, and other electronic games; younger crowd. Victoria House is a casual restaurant overlooking Lake Stieger serving a full menu of steaks, chops, chicken, shrimp, burgers, and sandwiches. Often full with Twin Citians on Saturday nights. Public golf course.

Phone

Lowry Nature Center	(612) 472-4911
Lake Auburn Campground	(612) 443-2911
Victoria House	(612) 443-2858
Deer Run Golf Course	(612) 443-2351
Victoria City Hall	(612) 443-2363

Get There   From central Minneapolis, take Interstate 394 west to U.S. Highway 169, then south on 169 to State Highway 7, then west on 7 approximately 17 miles to County Road 11. Turn left onto 11 and go about one mile to the park entrance on your left.

From south of Minneapolis, take Interstate 494 west to State Highway 5, then continue on 5 for approximately twelve miles and make a right turn onto Park Drive. Parking is about one-half mile ahead.

Carver Park Reserve

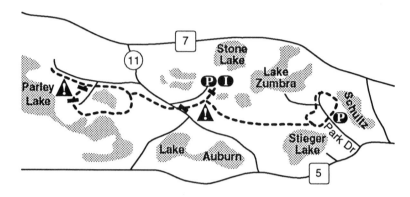

⚠️**Caution** The three-to-four-mile section of the trail that connects the Lowry Nature Center to County Road 11 is paved but rough – watch for infrequent autos. The short (0.3 mile) road on the northwest corner of the western loop was resurfaced in the summer of 1991 but is unskateable; it may improve with use. This section can be avoided by backtracking around the loop or reconnecting with the trail by walking across the picnic area.

It occurs to Skip that perhaps the more expensive pair would have been better.

13 Cleary Lake Regional Park
Clearly Nice

There are more skaters than bikers here and the wide path provides an ample margin for the gyrating young ones. A nice combination consists of the parents playing a round of golf while the kids skate.

Where   Twenty miles south of Minneapolis, just southwest of Prior Lake

Length   3.5 miles

Difficulty   *Beginner.* Flat with only gradual curves. Good for the whole family.

Surface   Good. Smooth, with very few cracks across the fifteen-foot-wide asphalt although there are two rough spots.

Terrain   Trail wraps around Cleary Lake, passing mostly through open prairie and a few wooded areas surrounding the lake. Mainly flat with gentle curves.

Facilities

Parking   Ample at the park pavilion and at the recreation center

Restrooms   Clubhouse, park pavilion (on beach)

Food   Snack bar in on-site clubhouse

Camping   Eight locations including one on Cleary Island

Picnic Sites   Lakeside areas; picnic pavilion available by reservation, spring, summer, fall

Fishing   Non-motorized boat launch

Golf   Eighteen-hole executive short course

Rentals   Skates, $4/hour including use of safety gear. Skate renters are required to wear helmets. Also bike rentals.

Phone   Picnic and campsite reservations   (612) 559-9000
              Golf course, recreation center   (612) 447-2171

Get There From Minneapolis, go south on Interstate 35W approximately 17 miles, then west on County Road 42 for 4 miles, and south on County Road 27 for 3.5 miles. The entrance is on your right.

From west of the Twin Cities, take Interstate 494 to U.S. Highway 169, then south about seven miles on 169 to State Highway 101. Take 101 east eight miles to State Highway 13, then south on 13 two miles to County Road 42, east on 42 three-quarters of a mile to County Road 27, and south on 27 3.5 miles to the park entrance on your right.

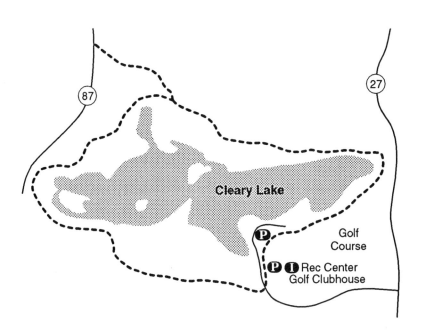

14 Como Park Zoo Parade

This is an especially great family trail because of the additional recreational activities nearby. The area can be crowded on summer weekends, but still worth the trip, which is so convenient for Twin Citians.

Where St. Paul, north of Interstate 94 and west of Interstate 35E; a short distance east of the Minnesota State Fairgrounds

Length 1.8 miles around Lake Como and 3.5 miles total, including path to Como Zoo and back

Difficulty *Beginner.* Flat; good for the whole family. Bicyclists and skaters are on a separate path from others, all going in the same direction.

Surface Excellent

Terrain Flat with the exception of gradual hills along the west side near the golf course. Surrounded by beautiful homes and Como Park. The extension to the zoo, which is three-quarters of a mile, begins at the main parking lot and takes you through a wooded area.

Facilities

Parking Ample free parking on northwest side of Lake Como

Restrooms In the pavilion on the northwest side of the lake

Food Snack food wagons outside the pavilion. The golf course has a cafeteria-style restaurant.

Pavilion Musical concerts held several times weekly during the summer. Building is available for daily rental; contact St. Paul Parks for permit. New pavilion to be completed spring 1992.

Nearby Como Zoo is open daily all year; no admission fee.

Formal Japanese gardens open May through August

The Conservatory has five different live-plant display areas that are open daily all year and a gift shop. Admission: 50¢ adults, 25¢ seniors and children.

Eighteen-hole public golf course

Amusement park operates during summer months only. Primarily children's rides.

Phone   St. Paul Parks and Recreation   (612) 488-7291
              Como Zoo   (612) 488-4041
              Conservatory   (612) 489-1740
              Como Golf Course   (612) 488-9679

Get There   Take Interstate 94 east from Minneapolis approximately five miles, or west from St. Paul about three miles; exit north onto Lexington Avenue. Go about two miles and veer to the right into the parking lot on the northwest side of Lake Como.

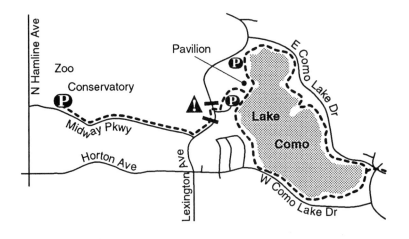

⚠ Caution   Extra control is required on the extension leading to the zoo since it crosses busy Lexington Avenue.

15 Douglas State Trail
Mayo – No Nays

While in Mayo Clinic country, take time to enjoy this challenging twenty-five mile round trip, but keep in mind the gravel road crossings and the slight hills leading to them. Not too heavily traveled.

Where   Between Rochester and Pine Island, 70 miles southeast of Minneapolis

Length   12.5 miles

Difficulty *Intermediate.* Gravel road crossings, wooden bridges.

Surface   Excellent. Resurfaced in 1987.

Terrain   Mostly a straight, flat route that takes skaters through meadows and farm country (the heartland, you know), as well as some wooded areas. The trail crosses over wooden bridges above the Zumbro River and Plum Creek.

Facilities

Parking   Ample parking available at all three access points

Restrooms Portables are located at the Rochester access point. Permanent restrooms are located in Douglas and Pine Island Park.

Food   Approximately two miles from the Pine Island access point is a soft drink machine and picnic table.

A small concession stand and country store are located in Douglas next to the trail. Hand-pumped well water is also available.

The Rochester access point does not provide food or beverages.

Picnic Site A sheltered picnic area, a ball field, and a horseshoe pit (no horseshoes provided) are located in Pine Island Park.

Nearby   Burgers and pizza are served at Johnny B's, and cocktails at the municipal bar; both are on Main Street in Pine Island.

The Mayo Clinic, if necessary.

Phone Rochester Trails and
    Waterways Unit, DNR   (507) 285-7176
    Pine Island Visitor Information   (507) 356-4591

Get There *Pine Island access.* From the Twin Cities, follow U.S. Highway 52 south to the Pine Island (County Road 11) exit. Proceed west for one-half mile, passing the haunted cemetery and entering Pine Island Park in which the trail begins.

Douglas access. Take U.S. Highway 52 to the County Road 14 exit. Proceed west to milepost 5.

Rochester access. Go 2 miles west on County Road 4, from the junction of U.S. Highway 52 and 4, to the parking lot on your right.

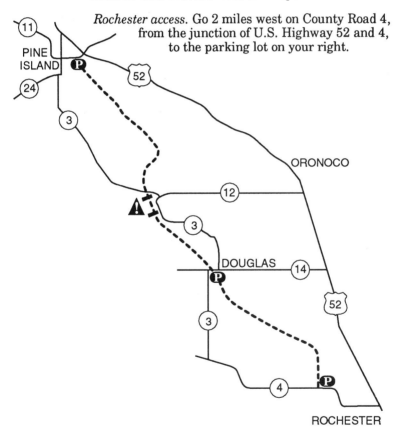

⚠ **Caution** There are several gravel roads and a few wooden bridges, including the one marked on the map, that require careful crossing.

16 Duluth-Carlton Segment of Willard Munger State Trail
Cooke Out

This is a remote, wilderness trail with beautiful scenery. Keep in mind that access to the route is limited along the way so you should be prepared to go the distance, bringing ample food and water. You may want to avoid the crowds during Grandma's Marathon in June.

Where   Duluth, 150 miles north of Minneapolis

Length   14.5 miles

Difficulty *Intermediate.* A few curves and steeper hills.

Surface   Excellent. Last surfaced in 1987, major reparation in 1991. Subject to cracking from washouts after heavy rainstorms and to cuts from falling rocks.

Terrain   Old resurfaced railroad bed with a one degree downhill grade from Carlton to Duluth. The trail winds through enchanted forests and alongside jagged rocks and several streams, crossing over a bridge that provides a spectacular view of the gorge underneath. Near Duluth, the view of Lake Superior is magnificent. At the Carlton end, the trail passes through Jay Cooke State Park.

Facilities

Parking   Ample parking available at both ends of the trail

Restrooms In the town of Carlton and near the Duluth access in several gas stations and restaurants.

Food   There are no treats along the trail but there are concession stands on the trail in Carlton. Food is also available, of course, in the cities of Carlton and Duluth.

Camping   There are two camping areas. One is located at the Duluth access point and the other is approximately 2.5 miles from the Carlton access point in Jay Cooke State Park.

Nearby   The trail takes you through Jay Cooke State Park
where you may want to take off the skates and go on
a hiking side trip. Carlton has a few local watering
holes, the Cozy Cafe and the Third Base Bar. Of
course you can always head into Duluth for more,
including a test of your luck at the casino.

DULUTH   There are several hotels in the Duluth area including Fitger's Inn, which offers a delightful view of
Lake Superior.

As a special note, we mention that the Willard Motel
at the Duluth trailhead is owned and operated by
state legislator Willard Munger whose name graces
the longest trail in Minnesota and who is perhaps
the legislature's prime proponent of recreational
trail development.

Fitger's Brewery Complex, 600 East Superior Street,
six blocks east of the Lake Avenue exit from Interstate 35, has lodging, dining, and shopping. Fitger's
Brewery is listed in the National Register of Historic
Places.

Glensheen, the haunted Congdon Mansion, 3300
London Road, is a 7.5 acre estate that was completed
in 1908. Guided and self-guided house tours are
available from 9:00 A.M. - 4:00 P.M. Admission is $6
for adults, $4.50 for senior citizens and $2.50 for stu-
dents, children, and University of Minnesota
employees. A grounds pass costs $3.

CARLTON   Superior white water rafting trips begin in Carlton,
3.4 miles east of Interstate 35 on State Highway
210, 20 miles south of Duluth. The trip takes about
2.5 hours. You need to be at least twelve years old
and in good health to withstand the power of the St.
Louis River. The cost is $29 per rafter and $49 per
inflatable kayak.

Duluth-Carlton Segment

Phone   Mooselake Trails and
                Waterways Unit, DNR   (218) 485-8647
                Fitger's Inn   (218) 722-8826 and 1-800-726-2982
                Glensheen   (218) 724-8864
                Rafting reservations   (218) 384-4637

Get There   *Duluth access.* Take Interstate 35 to Duluth and
                take exit 251B onto Grand Avenue (State Highway
                23 West). Follow Grand south for approximately one
                mile until you see signs that identify the trail. Turn
                left on 72nd Avenue at the Willard Motel. Parking is
                available on the right side after crossing the railroad
                tracks.

                Carlton access. Take Interstate 35 to State Highway
                210 and go east to Carlton. At the four-way stop,
                turn right onto County Road 1 and go one block to
                the trail parking lot.

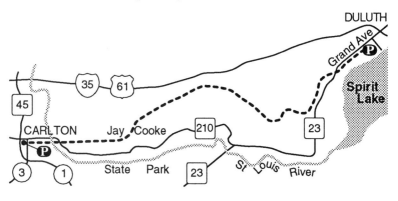

⚠ Caution   Beware of falling rocks as well as those already on
                the trail. Although the hills and curves are well
                marked with signs, treat them seriously.

52

Minnesota Moskato

The Skate *Bird*

17 Elm Creek Park Reserve
Picturesque

Mud and Goose lakes and their surrounding hills and trees create a beautiful backdrop for skating. Beginners might want to forgo the more challenging second half of the trail and spend some time at the beach or picnic site. Elm Creek connects to the 7.5 mile North Hennepin Trail Corridor (trail 36).

Where   Northwest of Osseo, between the communities of Champlain, Dayton, and Maple Grove

Length   Perimeter loop: 7.3 miles
                Figure 8:   9.3 miles

Difficulty *Advanced* due to the steep hills (some with wooden bridges at the bottoms) and curves that dominate the western half of the trail. The eastern loop is much less challenging.

Surface   Excellent

Terrain   The trail circles Mud and Goose lakes, amid woods, marshland, and meadows. The hills (if you can make it up them) allow skaters to view the full beauty of the area, particularly the picturesque scenes overlooking Mud Lake.

Facilities

Parking   Ample at east end of trail, near the beach

Restrooms   At visitor center and at the picnic and beach area

Food   Snacks available at the visitor center (weekends) and at the beach area (every day).

Picnic Site   Complete facilities, very large playground area, and swimming

Rentals   Available at the visitor center: croquet, bocceball, volleyball, horseshoes, skis, and bikes. Call for prices.

Nearby   Dairy Queen and Wendy's on County Road 81 just off Interstate 94. Cub Foods farther down 81.

                Northwest Inn (a Best Western) at 94 and 81

Phone	Eastman Nature Center	(612) 420-4300
	Visitor center	(612) 424-5511

Get There From downtown Minneapolis, go west about 11 miles on Interstate 94 to County Road 81, north 5.5 miles to Territorial Road, then right 3 blocks. Make a right turn into the reserve. The recreation center parking lot is about one-third mile inside.

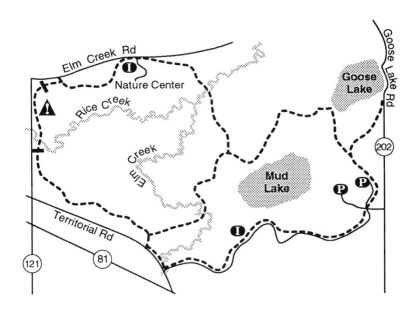

⚠**Caution** Although the path veers off in many directions, it is well marked so that skaters know exactly where they are headed. The most difficult section runs along County Road 121 and contains a steep hill with a bridge at the bottom.

18 Fish Lake Regional Park
Two Short

There are two short trails in the park, Bay Point and Glacial Ridge. After mastering the parking lot, either of these paths would be excellent for a public debut.

Where   Maple Grove, approximately fifteen miles west of Minneapolis

Length   Bay Point   0.5 mile
               Glacial Ridge   1 mile

Difficulty *Beginner*

Surface   Excellent

Terrain   Bay Point borders Fish Lake and is flat but Glacial Ridge weaves through woods and swampland over a few hills.

Facilities

Parking   Ample parking south of the visitor center

Restrooms   At the visitor center

Food   There are picnic tables and a concession stand at the visitor center.

Picnic Site   Near the beach area

Other   Skates and the required protective gear can be rented for $4 per hour at the visitor center.

Phone   Fish Lake Park
               4500 Bass Lake Road
               Maple Grove MN 55369
               (612) 420-3423

Get There From Minneapolis, take Interstate 94 west to Interstate 494, then south to Bass Lake Road (County Road 10 exit). Travel west on Bass Lake for one mile and turn right, into the park entrance.

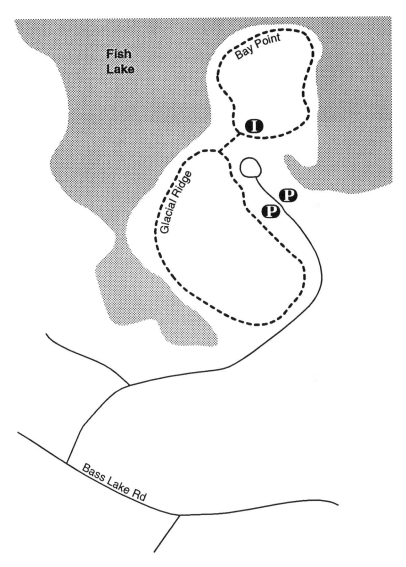

Fish Lake

Bay Point

Glacial Ridge

Bass Lake Rd

⚠ **Caution** Traffic can be heavy on weekends.

19 Fort Snelling State Park
Fortifying Frolic

A secret spot that provides scenic skating in historic surroundings within the metropolitan area. Skating is also allowed on the roadway. Along the river or lake you might come across white-tailed deer, foxes, woodchucks, badgers, skunks, and snapping, soft-shelled, or wood turtles – all basking in the sun.

Where   Southern Metro area near Minneapolis–St. Paul International Airport

Length   5 miles

Difficulty *Advanced*, but less experienced skaters can skate up to the fort and back, avoiding the steep hill at the fort.

Surface   Excellent

Terrain   A moderately hilly and curvy trail that traverses both wooded and open areas as it follows the Minnesota River past Snelling Lake under the Mendota Bridge, then along the Mississippi River, eventually connecting to the Minnehaha Creek trail (trail 32).

Facilities

Parking   At the park entrance

Restrooms At the park entrance, at Snelling Lake, and at the base of the fort

Food   Snacks and soft drinks at the park entrance

Picnic Sites 150 picnic sites with shelters

Other   Swimming beach and changing rooms at Snelling Lake. River and lake fishing. Boat and canoe landing at Snelling Lake. Polo grounds and golf course, as well as football, baseball, and soccer fields.

Markers   Historic Fort Snelling was the first outpost in the Northwest Frontier. Completed in 1824, it regulated the fur trade. Within the fort's walls are the first school, the first hospital, and the first library in Minnesota. The fort served as a training base and supply depot during the Civil War as well as World War II.

Phone   Fort Snelling State Park   (612) 725-2390

Get There Take Interstate 494 east towards the airport, staying on State Highway 5 and exiting at Post Road. Follow the signs into the park entrance.

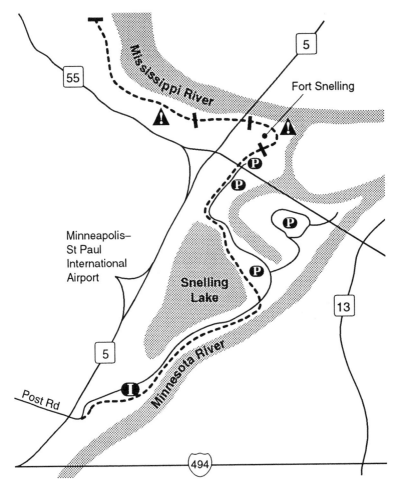

⚠ Caution There is a steep hill leading up to the fort. The part of the path connecting to the Minnehaha Creek trail (trail 32) has sharp curves and significant hills.

20 French Regional Park
Viva La Skate

A short path whose northern segment is suitable for experienced skaters wanting a quick workout. Beginners would do well to use nearby Fish Lake Regional Park. The southern loop can be hazardous due to frequent tram shuttle traffic.

Where	In Plymouth, on the north side of Medicine Lake
Length	1.75 miles
Difficulty	*Intermediate.* Hilly northern segment and tram traffic on the southern loop.
Surface	Excellent
Terrain	The southern loop bordering Medicine Lake is wooded and rather flat but the northern segment is winding and more hilly.

Facilities

Parking	At park central and also on east side of the southern loop
Restrooms	At the outdoor recreation center
Food	Snack bar at the recreation center
Other	Canoe rentals, playground, and swimming in Medicine Lake

Phone	French Regional Park	(612) 559-8891
Get There	Take Interstate 394 west from Minneapolis to U.S. Highway 169. Go north on 169 for about 3 miles to the County Road 9 exit. Travel west for 2.5 miles to the French Regional Park entrance, which is the first left after Larch Lane.	

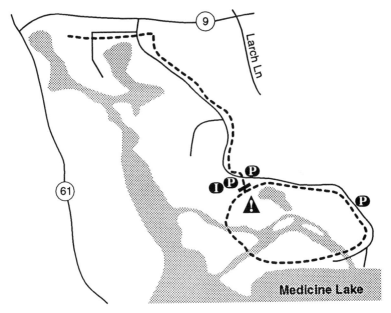

⚠ **Caution** The tram shuttle that makes frequent trips around the southern loop creates a major interference for skaters by taking up almost the whole width of the path.

21 Gateway Segment of Willard Munger State Trail
Brand New

Because this is a brand new trail, there may not be as much traffic as on other Metro area paths, but this trail is a real pearl – it will be discovered and coveted by many. By fall 1992, an additional 9.7 miles is expected to be completed, taking the path to Pine Point Park, four miles north of Stillwater. The eventual hope is to extend the trail all the way to Duluth.

Where Starting two miles north of St. Paul between Lake Como and Lake Phalen and extending east to Interstate 694 in Oakdale

Length 7.2 miles

Difficulty *Beginner.* Straight and flat.

Surface Excellent. Paving was begun in 1991 and completed in spring 1992. There are some rough spots in the 1.5 mile section between Arlington and Keller Park because an experimental surface material was used. This section will probably be repaved in 1993.

Terrain Converted railroad bed that weaves through both commercial and residential areas. Fairly open and flat with only gradual curves. The first 2.5 miles through residential neighborhoods is the most scenic part. The section from Interstate 694 to north of Stillwater is expected to be completed in the fall of 1992 and will be surrounded by contrasting landscapes of open meadows and wooded patches with an abundance of wildlife.

Facilities

Parking Free parking at west end, fee for parking at east end

Restrooms Portables at both parking lots, and restrooms along the way at commercial establishments

Food South of the Gateway trail, on the Phalen-Keller trail (trail 38) at the Phalen Beach House, pavilion, and Lakeside Activity Center. An assortment of fast food restaurants are located near the east end, along State Highway 36.

Phone   Metro Region Headquarters of DNR (612) 772-7935

Get There *West end of trail.* From St. Paul take Interstate 35E north to the Maryland Avenue exit and go one block east on Maryland to Westminster Street. Go north on Westminster to Arlington Avenue, east on Arlington one block, and turn left into the parking lot.

East end of (completed) trail. Take State Highway 36 to Hadley Avenue North, about one-third mile west of Interstate 694. Go south on Hadley and make an immediate left onto the frontage road. Parking lot is one-half mile ahead on your right.

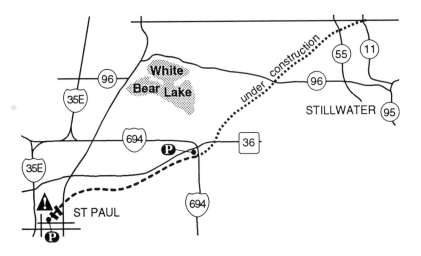

⚠ **Caution** The trail crosses several streets and roads. Specially constructed bridges span the more heavily traveled thoroughfares and most create no problem to crossing. Special attention, however, should be given to the bridge over Westminster Street at the west end of the trail where there is a slight step on each side.

22 Heartland State Trail
Eat Your Heart Out

First blacktopped trail in the country. You will definitely not starve on this trail. A lunch stop in Dorset would be memorable no matter which of its eateries you chose. Dorset has been called "The Restaurant Capital of the World" because it has thirty-five residents and four restaurants. Be sure to pick up a copy of the *Dorset Daily Bugle* – published once a year! This is resort country with many cozy places to stay, many arts and crafts shops to enjoy.

Where   Between State Highway 34 in Park Rapids and Cass County Road 12 in Walker

Length   27 miles

Difficulty   *Beginner.* Very flat and straight.

Surface   Satisfactory. Narrow, only six-feet wide. Consideration is being given to resurfacing. There is a short, especially rough section, one mile east of Dorset.

Terrain   Generally flat and straight. Converted railroad bed. Quite wooded from Park Rapids to Nevis. Especially pretty area crossing Shallow Lake between Dorset and Nevis. At Nevis, State Highway 34 parallels the trail until about two miles east of Akeley at which point the most scenic section begins, ending at Walker. Wooded areas with many lakes.

Facilities

Parking   Lots at Park Rapids and Walker have free overnight parking. On-street parking in Dorset, Nevis, and Akeley.

Restrooms   Numerous along the trail

Food:

DORSET   Four colorful restaurants, all on Main Street: Compadres Del Norte, Dorset Cafe, Dorset House, and Woodstock North

NEVIS   Cookie Jar Bakery and Coffee Shop
Schleicher's Steakhouse
Shenanigan's
Liquid refreshments at Lounge and Bar

AKELEY Yodelin Swedes is a local tavern with pre-made pizza, sandwiches, and pool tables. Probably unsuitable for impressing CEO of Dayton's.

Shirley's Cafe and Restaurant

WALKER The Bar and Restaurant at the Chase Hotel (on Leech Lake) is a great spot for dinner. Moderate prices, nice casual attire recommended. More casual in the bar during the day.

The Wharf is an attractive restaurant and bar located on Main Street.

Picnic Sites Numerous picnic areas available in all four cities

Nearby Perhaps the region's most notable landmark is the huge Paul Bunyan statue located on Main Street, one block off the trail in Akeley. Be sure to have your picture taken sitting on Paul's hand.

Bluebird Trail from Park Rapids to Akeley has been created by maintaining 110 bird houses along the trail.

Nevis claims to be home of the world's largest replica Tiger Muskie. It is displayed on Main Street.

Park Rapids and Walker have ample accommodations.

Phone Park Rapids Chamber of Commerce
Park Rapids MN 56470
(218) 732-4111

Leech Lake Area Chamber of Commerce
Walker MN 56484
(218) 547-1313

DNR Heartland Trail Headquarters
P.O. Box 112
Nevis MN 56467
(218) 652-4054

Heartland State Trail

Get There In Park Rapids, go east on State Highway 34 to the city center, and turn left (north) on Central Avenue (semaphore at intersection). There is a sign on Central pointing to the trail, which is approached from your left.

In Walker, take State Highway 34 east to State Highway 371, and turn left onto 371 (heading north) for one block. There is a sign on the left pointing to the trail. Make a left turn off 371.

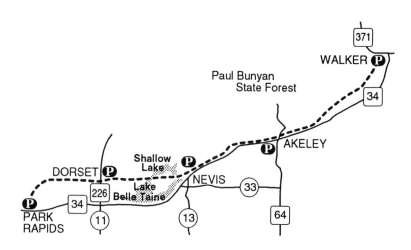

⚠ Caution The narrowness of the path necessitates extra awareness of approaching skaters and bikers. Numerous road crossings, some paved but most gravel.

Weak end skating

23 Hidden Falls / Crosby Farm
Your Falls Won't Be Hidden

This is a great place to skate because most of the other bikers and walkers are exercising on the River Road path, which runs above this trail at the top of the Mississippi River embankment. Crosby Farm and Hidden Falls are little known. If you want to get away from the noise and exhaust, come down to the lazy river.

Where Highland Park area of St. Paul, on the Mississippi River

Length 5 miles

Difficulty *Intermediate*. Hills and curves.

Surface Satisfactory

Terrain The trail runs along the Mississippi River, over small hills, around gentle curves and through sunny and shaded areas. The Crosby Farm segment contains a few more curves but fewer people are found on the path in these beautiful woods. The trail also passes limestone caves and circles around Crosby Lake. Speed can be controlled because the small hills are followed by flat terrain.

Facilities

Parking Ample free parking available at all access points. The park is open from sunrise to 10:00 P.M.

Restrooms At two pavilions and at portables throughout the park

Food There are no treats along the trail. Refreshments can be found from other people's picnic baskets or you will need to travel in a car to Highland Park or to West Seventh Street for fast food.

Camping No overnight camping

Picnic Sites Picnic sites available throughout both parks. Grills are available at no charge – just bring your own charcoal and lighting fluid. Covered shelter is available at a pavilion within each park.

Nearby   The Ford Dam is a worthy site. A visit to the monument at Summit and Mississippi River Boulevard offers the opportunity to climb down the river bank for a peaceful break.

Phone   St. Paul Parks and Recreation   (612) 292-7400

Get There Take Interstate 94 to Cretin Avenue and go south to Summit Avenue, then west (right) on Summit towards the river. Two blocks later, turn left at the stop sign onto Mississippi River Boulevard and go a few miles south past the Ford Bridge and the Ford Dam. The North Gate entrance is on your right.

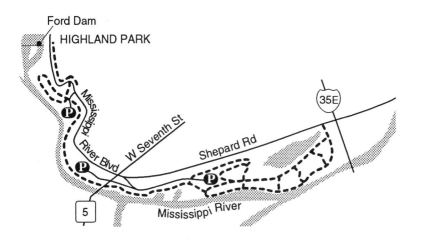

⚠ Caution Because the Crosby Farm part of the trail is very wooded, there is a greater than normal presence of leaves and twigs. Shaded areas in Crosby are very damp and quite slick after a rain.

24 Hinckley-Barnum Segment of Willard Munger State Trail
Fire Up!

You might want to skate only parts of this thirty-seven-mile trail running between Hinckley and Barnum. It will be even longer when completed and connected to the Duluth-Carlton segment. This is a terrific trail to practice on while you become comfortable on skates; perfect for beginning skaters because of its light use.

Where	Hinckley, seventy miles north of the Twin Cities
Length	37 miles
Difficulty	*Beginner.* Flat and mostly straight.
Surface	Excellent. The Hinckley to Moose Lake section was paved in 1985, Moose Lake to Barnum in 1990.
Terrain	For the most part, flat and straight, lying on an old railroad bed. Runs through farmland and some wooded areas, and by small towns and meadows.

Facilities

Parking	In Hinckley, Finlayson, Willow River, Moose Lake, and Barnum
Restrooms	Available at all parking sites and small towns along the way
Food	Restaurants in Hinckley, Finlayson, Willow River, Moose Lake, and Barnum

Nearby

HINCKLEY The Hinckley Fire Museum reveals everything concerning the Great Hinckley Fire of 1894. The fire destroyed thousands of acres and six towns, driving the residents of Hinckley to dive into Skunk Lake in order to escape the blaze that surrounded them.

A casino is being built and will be finished in spring 1992.

Tobie's serves its famous caramel rolls and beverages. You can also stop and play a round of miniature golf or visit Bohn's Petting Zoo located behind Tobie's.

FINLAYSON The Municipal Bar offers a drink and a game of pool, after which you might head to the Old Fashion Inn for some home-cooked food.

The Victoria Rose (a bed and breakfast listed in the National Register of Historic Places) was built by John Oldenberg, a land purchaser for the railroad, in 1896. Open on weekends.

WILLOW RIVER Picnic sites and the Mercantile Old Fashion Store for antiques and food

RUTLEDGE 100-year-old town that used to be the home of the state's largest sawmill

MOOSE LAKE Agate capital of the world and gateway to arrowhead country. A variety of restaurants and bars where you can eat, drink, and be merry.

BARNUM Site of Carlton County Fair, mid-August. Restaurant and bar in town.

Phone Moose Lake Trails and
Waterway Unit, DNR   (218) 485-8647

Get There From the Twin Cities, take Interstate 35 north, exit on State Highway 48 (Tobie's exit), and head west on 48 for about three-quarters of a mile to Old Highway 61. Turn right and go about three-quarters of a mile, passing a Dairy Queen, to Second Street. Turn left on Second, go over the railroad tracks, and turn right into the trail parking lot.

Hinckley-Barnum Segment

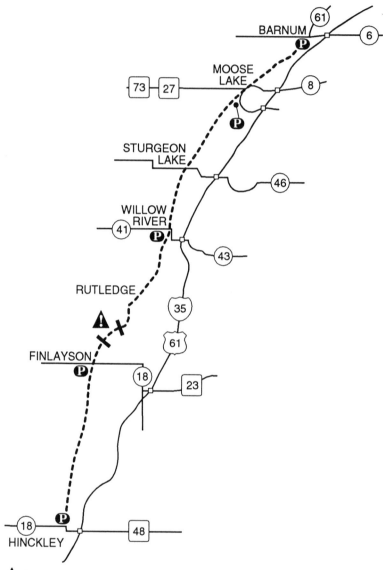

⚠ Caution The trail crosses roads at various points where cars and gravel can present hazards. The section that is equidistant from Rutledge and Finlayson leaves the railroad bed and is quite hilly.

Wrong Rollers

25 Hyland Lake Park Reserve
Endeering

This path winds through very pretty scenery in a park that contains a large population of deer and Canadian geese. The whole family will enjoy the extensive playground including its huge slide, Chutes and Ladders. The trail is fairly heavily used but is adequate to the traffic.

Where West Bloomington, in the general area bounded by Interstate 494 on the north, Old Shakopee Road on the south, Bush Lake Road on the west, and Normandale Boulevard on the east.

Length 5.75 miles

Difficulty *Intermediate.* A few steep hills.

Surface Good

Terrain The trail is comprised of three interconnected loops that pass through some wooded areas along mostly rolling prairie. There are long, gradually inclined stretches as well as a few short steep hills. The path runs along the western and southern edges of Hyland Lake.

Facilities

Parking Ample, both at the lot in Hyland Park and at the boat launch at Bush Lake Park.

Restrooms At the Richardson Nature Center and the recreation center

Food Snack shop and water in the recreation center

Picnic Sites In addition to the picnic tables along the trail, there is a large picnic area near the recreation center.

Playground Near the recreation center is an exceptional playground – its primary attraction is the giant slide.

Other Fishing is available at Hyland Lake and across the road at Bush Lake.

Nearby *Richardson Nature Center.* Located about two miles north of the park entrance on East Bush Lake Road. The wood-chip trails are enjoyable to walk but are unskateable, of course.

Phone   Recreation center   (612) 941-4362
                 Entrance gate   (612) 944-9882
                 Richardson Nature Center   (612) 941-7993

Get There   Take Interstate 494 to Normandale Boulevard, then south to West 84th Street. Stay on West 84th as it turns into East Bush Lake Road and curves south about two miles. The park entrance is on your left.

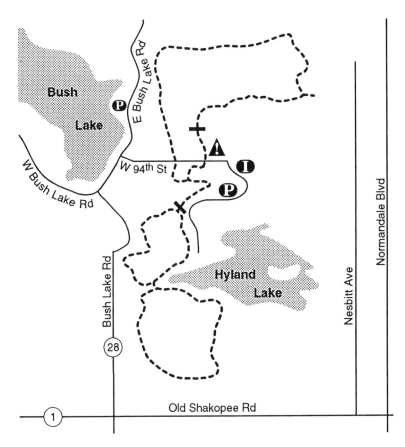

⚠ Caution   The most stressful and dangerous area is the long downhill run near the middle loop that crosses the park entrance road at a place where many skaters will have built up speed. Care should be taken to maintain control in this region.

26 Itasca State Park
Mississippi Mission

Perhaps the most scenic trail in Minnesota, it also offers unique historical experiences. Itasca State Park is located at the headwaters of the Mississippi River where it begins its 2,552-mile journey to the Gulf of Mexico. Heavy traffic during the summer. The fall foliage is especially beautiful.

Where   Twenty miles north of Park Rapids on U.S. Highway 71. In three counties: Clearwater, Hubbard, and Becker.

Length   17 miles. 6.5 miles of off-road path and 10.5 miles on Wilderness Drive, most of which is a low-traffic, one-way road.

Difficulty   The off-road part is *intermediate*; good-sized hills with some blind curves. The Wilderness Trail is *advanced*; long, moderately steep hills require extra control in order to avoid cars and bikes.

Surface   Good. The eight-foot wide off-road blacktop is acceptably smooth but has some cracks. Just north of the campgrounds (about halfway through the trail), there is a short rough section.

The off-road segment terminates at the headwaters where there is a seventy-five-foot walk over a sand and gravel road in order to get to the parking lot that exits to Wilderness Drive.

Wilderness Drive starts out as a smooth two-way road and continues for about 3.5 miles at which point it changes into a wide one-way road for the final seven miles.

Terrain   The off-road section consists of gradual curves and hills with most downhill parts followed by gradual uphill grades that break your speed. The tall pines and lakes, especially the largest lake – Itasca – provide spectacular scenery.

Facilities

Parking   Parking lots available at South Itasca Center, Mississippi Headwaters, and midway on the off-road trail at the campgrounds

Restrooms   Numerous, including those at Douglas Lodge, Forest Inn, Brower Inn, the campgrounds, and the Headwaters Gift Shop

Picnic Sites   Several along the trail and one large picnic grounds three-quarters of a mile south of the headwaters

Other   The park offers visitors a variety of interesting things to see and do. Near the South Itasca Center (southeast end of the trail) is the Douglas Lodge, a historic log hotel overlooking Lake Itasca, with food service, rooms, and cabin rental. From late May through September, the dining room is open from 7:30 A.M. to 8:00 P.M. daily. Several boat landings and boat tours are available through the lodge.

Across from the Douglas Lodge is the log and stone Forest Inn, which has a gift shop, interpretive programs, and a meeting room.

On the off-road trail, about one mile south of the headwaters, is the Brower Inn, which consists of two snack bars.

Markers   There are many historical markers interspersed along the trail, including the following.

Preacher's Grove is located about one mile north of the start of the off-road segment and named for a religious convention that once camped there. The stand of more than 250-year-old Red Pine began growing after a major fire in 1714.

Peace Pipe Vista is situated 1.5 miles farther down the trail, providing a wide-angle view of Lake Itasca. A favorite spot to take pictures, watch the sun set, and listen to the evening loons.

The Natural History Museum is a wildlife treasury located about one mile south of the headwaters.

Just east of the headwaters lie five-hundred year old Indian Mounds burial sites that were partially excavated in 1890 and are now protected by law from further disturbance.

The Bison Site is the location of archaeological studies establishing that people were present in this area 8,000 years ago.

Nearby
The twenty miles between Park Rapids and Itasca contain numerous motels, cabins, and resorts as well as two golf courses.

Deertown, located just north of Park Rapids, has shops and a fenced-in area with native deer.

The Rapid River Logging Camp has good family-style food.

Summerhill Farm is a great lunch spot with arts and crafts shops.

There are abundant one-half- to three-mile-long hiking trails in the region.

Over 200 campsites exist in the area including drive-in types as well as backpack campsites.

Phone
Itasca State Park Manager
Lake Itasca MN 56460
(218) 266-3654
For accommodations: 1-800-765-CAMP (2267)

Get There
Enter the park at either the South Entrance (left off U.S. Highway 71, north onto County Road 1) or the East Entrance (left off Highway 71, north onto State Highway 200, then left onto County Road 48). Both will take you to the information booth and office at the South Itasca Center where the off-road trail starts.

Driving about six miles north on State Highway 200 from its junction with U.S. 71 will take you to County Road 2, which leads south into the North Entrance.

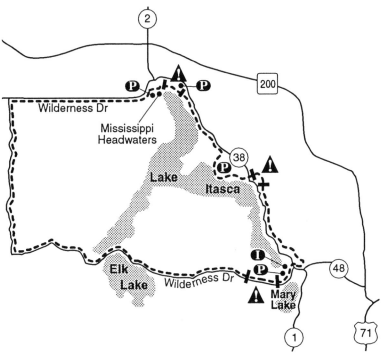

⚠ Caution The off-road segment crosses County Road 38 just beyond Peace Pipe Vista, about three miles into the trail. The approach to this stop is located around a curve on a gradual downhill slope but is well marked. After the crossing, there is a downhill slope with a subsequent uphill grade that is insufficient to stop you without braking.

The Wilderness Drive segment is hilly with sharp curves. Although most of the hills are similar in height and thus provide adequate speed control, the last half mile is almost all downhill ending with a sharp curve to the left. If not careful, you could end up in Mary Lake!

You may want to take advantage of being able to drive the Wilderness Trail in order to become familiar with it before skating.

27 Lake Cornelia
Ediner Inliner

Heavily used, but the wide range of facilities provides an exceptional family outing. The Art Center offers many interesting craft activities.

Where   Edina, just south of State Highway 62

Length   2.2 miles

Difficulty   *Beginner.* Excellent family path, but with two potentially difficult spots.

Surface   Good, with a few cracks

Terrain   Mostly flat with just a few curves and small hills. Path circles Lake Cornelia, passing by the Art Center. About one third of the trail cuts through woods; the rest of the scenery consists of marshland.

Facilities

Parking   Free parking by the swimming pool and by the picnic/play area.

Restrooms   At the pool and in the picnic area

Food   Concession stand at the pool – chips, pop, ice cream, popcorn, and so forth.

Picnic Site   Located at the northwest end: tables, shelter, barbecue, softball diamond, and children's play area. The tennis courts border the path.

Pool   Public wading and lap pools with a diving area

VitaCourse   Get an additional workout along the path.

Nearby   Southdale Shopping Center and the Galleria are within a couple of blocks. A Target store is located at 70th and York.

Phone   Edina Parks and Recreation   (612) 927-8861

Get There   Take State Highway 62 to the France Avenue exit. Go south two blocks to 66th Street then right on 66th for two more blocks, curving to the right onto Valley View Road. The entrance is one-half block ahead on your left. Drive around the pool and follow the signs to parking for the Art Center and trail.

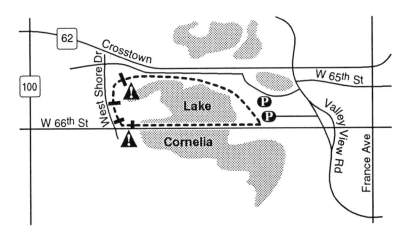

⚠ Caution   There are only two potentially difficult spots. By the Art Center at the northwest end, the trail curves left (skating counter clockwise) and takes what may be an unexpected downhill turn. At the southwest end, the path curves left going uphill and then runs parallel to West 66th Street.

28 Lake Rebecca Park Reserve
Swanny River

Shorebirds and waterfowl abound in the Reserve's restored and restocked wildlife ponds. You will enjoy observing the trumpeter swans that are being reintroduced into the area. Traffic is heaviest in the spring and early fall, but even at its peak is probably only one-tenth that of the more heavily used trails nearer the Twin Cities.

Where   In Rockford, approximately 28 miles west of Minneapolis

Length   6.5 miles including a 0.7 mile stretch connecting to County Road 50

Difficulty   *Intermediate.* There are some hills that provide a good workout but watch out for the blind curves.

Surface   Good. The blacktop is best on the east side of Lake Rebecca and somewhat rougher on the rest of the trail.

Terrain   Combination of wooded, lake areas and wide open prairie with some hills that offer scenic views.

Facilities

Parking   Ample parking located just inside park entrance. The two additional trail access points have only on-street parking.

Restrooms   At the picnic sites

Food   Just off the northeast corner of the reserve, down County Road 50 and one block east on Highway 55 is Billy Bob's Pub and Grub, in Greenfield. With caution, you can skate to it.

Picnic Sites   Several picnic areas along the trail. Three full service picnic sites capable of accommodating a total of 2500 people.

Rental   Bikes (helmets included), aqua bikes, row boats, canoes, paddle boats, volleyball/net, bocceball, horseshoes, and croquet

Other   Creative play area, swimming beach, boat launch, hiking trails, 7.5 mile horseback riding trail

Nearby   In Rockford, try the Main Street Bar or the cafe that is around the corner on Bridge Street.

About twelve miles east of Rockford is the Medina Ballroom serving food along with old-time, country, and rock entertainment.

Phone   Trailhead   (612) 972-2620
Picnic reservations   (612) 559-9000

Get There   From Minneapolis, go west on State Highway 55 past Hamel to County Road 50 in Rockford. Turn left (south); go about two miles on 50 and turn left into the park.

There are two non-motorized access points to the trail from County Road 50. One is prior to (north of) the reserve entrance, just off State Highway 55 after crossing the railroad tracks. The other is located one mile after (south of) the entrance.

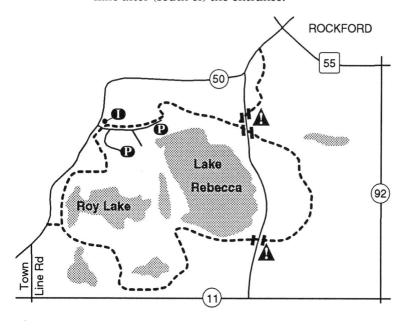

⚠ Caution   The hills and curves may be a problem for beginners, especially if there is significant bike traffic. The trail crosses a gravel road three times.

29 Long Lake Regional Park
Won't Take Long

A kinder and gentler trail that offers the choice of a circular route or a straight path that must be retraced.

Where	New Brighton, just north of Interstate 694 on the east side of Long Lake
Length	3 miles
Difficulty	*Beginner*. Flat and smooth surface.
Surface	Excellent
Terrain	Flat with some small inclines and a few curves as the trail winds through scenic woods alongside Long Lake

Facilities

Parking	Free parking on the left side, about one-third mile after entering the park and also at the beach house and the picnic pavilion
Restrooms	At the beach house, picnic pavilion, and Soo Line Depot museum
Picnic Sites	The picnic pavilion is open to family-sized parties without reservation and has kitchen facilities to accommodate reservations for groups up to 400. A few tables are also located along the trail.
Other	Beach house for swimming in Long Lake with adjacent playground. Fishing and boating on Long Lake. Soo Line Depot museum.

Phone	Ramsey County Parks and Recreation (612) 777-1707
Get There	From the Twin Cities, go north on Interstate 35W to State Highway 96. Head west on 96 to Old Highway 8 and proceed south on Old Highway 8 about 0.4 mile. Park entrance is on your right.

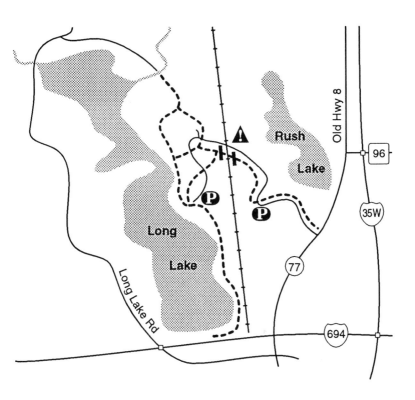

⚠ **Caution** The trail crosses railroad tracks midway on its southern segment.

30 Mendota Heights Trail
Women dota, too

Use this short, pretty trail to capture a taste of the country within the city.

Where   Mendota Heights, south of St. Paul

Length   1.75 miles

Surface   *Excellent*

Difficulty Beginner. Rolling hills.

Terrain   The trail begins by crossing a wooden footbridge over a small stream and entering a wooded area followed by open meadowland with patches of spruce and mixed hardwoods.

Facilities

Parking   Ample, in the lot off Marie Avenue

Restrooms In the picnic shelter near the parking lot

Food   None. Water available at the picnic shelter.

Other   Children's playground, tennis courts

Nearby   Varied dining and entertainment are available along State Highway 13.

Phone   City of Mendota Heights   (612) 452-1850

Get There   From Minneapolis, take State Highway 62 east across the Mendota Bridge. Stay to your left and enter State Highway 110 at the second stop light after the bridge. Stay on 110 for two miles until turning left at Dodd Road. Take Dodd about one-half mile and turn left onto Marie Avenue. The entrance is a few blocks ahead on your left.

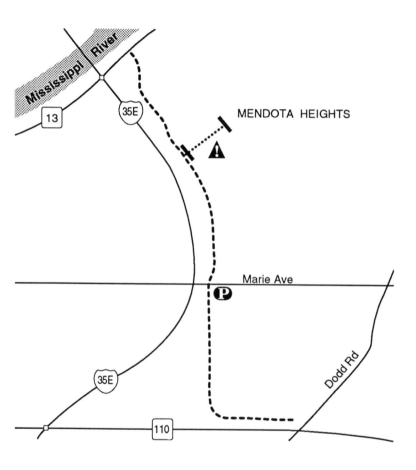

⚠️ Caution Avoid the spur midway on the trail leading up a steep hill to the right.

31 Minneapolis Central: Lake of the Isles, Calhoun, Harriet
Three's A Crowd

Isles, Calhoun, and Harriet are part of the extensive chain of waterways in the Minneapolis park system. The trails have a separate paved path for walkers and another for bikers and skaters, and are the only paths in the Minneapolis system where travel is one-directional (clockwise). Along the way you can enjoy special events like theater on the north side of Lake of the Isles, concerts at the Lake Harriet Bandshell, or even milk carton races at Lake Calhoun during the Minneapolis Aquatennial.

Where   Southwest Minneapolis

Length 10 miles

Lake of the Isles	3.0
Lake Calhoun	3.2
Lake Harriet	3.0
Calhoun-Harriet connection	0.8

Difficulty *Intermediate.* Crowded, especially on weekends.

Surface Satisfactory

Terrain The Lake of the Isles trail is mostly flat except for one hill on the west side of the Lake. You cruise past beautiful mansions with expansive front yards.

The Lake Calhoun path takes you around the lake and through tree-covered parks. Lots of grass for beginners and the weary. Also, people-watching, volleyball, frisbee, sailing, fishing, and windsurfing.

The Lake Harriet trail circles the lake amidst grass, trees, and large mansions. The whimsical, fairy tale refectory with its six flag-waving turrets received an architectural award.

Facilities

Parking Free on-street parking around all three lakes

Lake of the Isles has no parking lots. Lake Calhoun has several parking areas including North Beach on Lake Street (across from the Calhoun Beach Club) and Thomas Beach on the south end.

Lake Harriet has parking at the bandshell.

Restrooms   Portables located at several sites around all three lakes. Permanent facilities are also located at the Lake Calhoun concession stand and the Harriet bandshell.

Food   Refreshments at the concession stand on Lake Calhoun and at the refectory next to the bandshell at Lake Harriet. Fresh water pumps on all three lakes. If the vendors who pass through the area can't satisfy your palate, skate up Lake Street for a variety of cuisine.

Rentals   Several skate shops on West Lake Street where rentals are available by the hour or by the day. Rates are approximately $4-6 per hour, with reduced prices after one hour. Renting for the day costs $12-15. It is also possible to purchase used and new skates at these establishments:

Studio A, 1523 West Lake Street (612) 825-3077

Rolling Soles, 1700 West Lake Street at James Avenue (612) 823-5711

Cal-Surf, 1715 West Lake Street (612) 822-6840

Skate the Lakes, Calhoun Village on West Lake Street (612) 926-2019

Picnic Sites   Available throughout the parks. Grills are located at Lake Harriet; just bring your own charcoal and lighting fluid.

Benches are plentiful around all three lakes for resting and old-fashioned picnicking.

Beaches   Several locations with lifeguards at both Lake Calhoun and Lake Harriet. No swimming beaches at Lake of the Isles.

Nearby   Lake of the Isles is situated in the elegantly old Kenwood area of Minneapolis. Take off your skates and walk through the neighborhood, perhaps passing by the Mary Tyler Moore home.

At Lake Calhoun you can sit on any of the boat docks and enjoy a clear view of windsurfers and ducks.

The east side of Lake Harriet offers a walk through the rose garden or bird sanctuary for a peaceful respite from the noise and people. On the west side, visit the Linden Hills area for food, special coffee, and shopping.

A restored, fifties-vintage electric trolley carries passengers between Lake Harriet and Lake Calhoun past Lakewood Cemetery.

Phone   Minneapolis Parks and Recreation   (612) 348-2226

Get There   To get to Lake of the Isles from St. Paul, take Interstate 94 west to the Hennepin/Lyndale exit. Keep to the left, following the Hennepin exit signs, and take Hennepin to Franklin Avenue. Turn right (west) passing Sebastian Joe's ice cream shop to Lake of the Isles at Logan Avenue.

To get to Lake Calhoun from St. Paul, take Interstate 94 west proceeding as above but passing Franklin Avenue and continuing on Hennepin for about two miles until you reach Lagoon Avenue. Take a right on Lagoon (west) a few blocks to Lake Street. Calhoun is on your left side. Park anywhere.

To get to the east side of Lake Harriet, exit from Interstate 35W at 46th Street and head west about 1.5 miles to the lake.

⚠ Caution   Be wary of the hill on the west side of Lake of the Isles at the intersection of Lake of the Isles Parkway and Dean Parkway, but don't panic – it is surrounded by grass and followed by a flat stretch. Also be careful near the connecting path between Isles and Calhoun at 28th Street where the turn under the bridge is sharp and you need to gain some speed in order to get up the hill. There is two-way traffic here and some individuals skate and bike over the dividing lines.

There are two points of caution on the Calhoun segment. The first is a hill just after the bridge (the only bridge) along Lake Street located right before the snack bar and canoe rental area. The speed that is built up traveling down this hill and the poor surface at its bottom make stopping at the stop sign difficult. This point has been the scene of many accidents. The connecting trail to Lake of the Isles has two-way traffic and you will need to make a sharp turn going under the bridge.

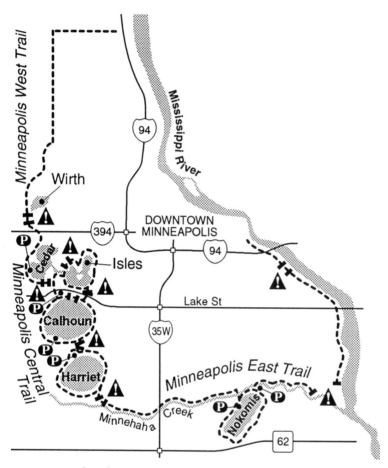

On the Lake Harriet segment, caution is required when traveling towards the bandshell and refectory, since that area is congested and you pass through a parking lot. Also there is a hill on the east side of the lake that should be approached with speed in order to avoid the need to walk with your skates on.

Note that the paths connecting Lake of the Isles with Lake Calhoun, and Lake Calhoun with Lake Harriet are two-way. The connecting path along William Berry Road between Calhoun and Harriet is a steep hill.

91

32 Minneapolis East: Minnehaha Creek, Lake Nokomis Parkway, West River Parkway
East Coasting

The Twin Cities Marathon, described widely as one of the most scenic in the nation, follows along a good portion of these trails, which are part of the 37.9-mile chain in the Minneapolis park system. Lake Nokomis and Minnehaha Parkway are quite popular on weekends but West River Parkway is far less congested.

Where   Southeast Minneapolis

Length   12.3 miles:

Minnehaha Creek	4.9 miles
Lake Nokomis Parkway	2.8 miles
West River Parkway	4.6 miles

Difficulty   *Intermediate.* Significant hills on West River Parkway and Minnehaha Creek but Lake Nokomis Parkway is really a beginner trail. Heavy skate and bike traffic.

Surface   Good. Some connecting segments are cement sidewalks. Skating in both directions with a separate walking path.

Terrain   The Minnehaha section curves through heavily wooded areas along Minnehaha creek until it joins Nokomis Parkway, which is more flat. West River Parkway is hilly, wooded, and affords beautiful views overlooking the Mississippi River.

Facilities

Parking   Available all along the twelve-mile trail on adjacent streets. There are several parking lots at Lake Nokomis.

Restrooms   Permanent restrooms are available at the Lake Nokomis Recreation Center, and portables can be found intermittently throughout the trail. Also gas stations and some fast food restaurants.

Food   Concession stands at Nokomis with a Dairy Queen across the street on Hiawatha. Vendors can be found along Minnehaha and Nokomis. Once you get to

West River Parkway you can turn off on Franklin and head west for several restaurants. Water pumps and faucets are located along the path.

Picnic Sites There are shelters and tables available at Lake Nokomis and Minnehaha Park. You can picnic almost anywhere along the trail. West River Parkway has benches with scenic views for an enjoyable rest. You can also venture towards the University of Minnesota and picnic on campus.

Beaches Lake Nokomis has a few beaches with lifeguard stations.

Nearby Minnehaha Parkway has markers that will point you to Minnehaha Falls Park, lying beyond Lake Nokomis, close to the Mississippi River. The park is a peaceful place to rest. Minnehaha Creek is fun for floating in an inner tube or small raft but the water level varies according to recent rainfall and might provide a rocky ride if too low.

Lake Nokomis offers tennis, baseball/softball fields, playgrounds, swimming, sunbathing, canoeing, and fishing.

You might enjoy taking West River Parkway to the West Bank of the University of Minnesota, then crossing the cement-paved bridge over the Mississippi and skating around the East Bank campus. From there, you can catch East River Parkway and skate down a steep hill leading to Riverside Park at which the University of Minnesota Showboat is docked. The pavement leaving the park toward St. Paul is very rough and unsuitable for skating.

Phone Minneapolis Parks and Recreation   (612) 348-2226

Get There You can join the Minnehaha Creek path by taking West 50th Street in south Minneapolis to Lynnhurst Park between Humboldt and James avenues.

Parking on the northwest side of Lake Nokomis can

93

be reached from Cedar Avenue South at its junction with West Lake Nokomis Parkway or by turning south from East Minnehaha Parkway as it skirts the north side of the lake.

There is parking along West River Road including just north of the Franklin Bridge in Riverside Park.

See Minneapolis map, page 91

⚠ **Caution** There is a steep hill on Minnehaha Parkway located just beyond West 50th Street as you skate from Lake Harriet – it should be walked, not skated, by the vast majority of us. This area is marked. The path also intersects several busy streets.

Currently, there is a missing half-mile section of trail at Godfrey Road between Minnehaha Avenue and West River Parkway. You can bypass this by using sidewalks and rejoining the trail at the Ford Bridge.

There is a very steep hill on West River Parkway near the Franklin Bridge that is followed by some flat terrain and an additional hill heading toward the West Bank of the University of Minnesota.

Thanks to their passion for in-line skating, Chip and Dale are about to discover a new meaning to the term male bonding.

33 Minneapolis West: Cedar Lake, Wirth, and Memorial Parkways
Wirth While

This part of the 37.9 mile chain of Minneapolis Park System trails has less activity than the others. Cedar Lake trail connects to both Lake of the Isles and Lake Calhoun trails (trail 31).

Where   Western Minneapolis

Length   8 miles

Cedar Lake Parkway	1.7 miles
Wirth Parkway	3.5 miles
Memorial Parkway	2.8 miles

Difficulty   *Intermediate.* Curvy, bumpy with several road crossings.

Surface   Satisfactory

Terrain   The path winds around the west side of Cedar Lake and then continues through Wirth and Memorial parks passing through woods and by lakes and ponds.

Facilities

Parking   On adjacent streets along the trail as well as in parking lots at Wirth and Memorial parks and Cedar Lake

Restrooms   Portables along the path and permanent ones at the Wirth concession area

Food   Concession stand at the north end of Wirth Park serving drinks and snacks

Fishing   Cedar Lake

Picnic Sites   Tables and shelters available throughout the trail

Beaches   Cedar Lake has two public beaches with lifeguard stations, one on the east end, the other on the south.

Other   Public golf course and driving range at Theodore Wirth Park. Also, the Eloise Butler Garden is a wildflower garden and bird sanctuary

Phone   Minneapolis Parks and Recreation   (612) 348-2226

Get There   Take State Highway 55 west from Minneapolis to Theodore Wirth Parkway and go south on Wirth past Glenwood Avenue to the parking lot on the right.

To connect to the Lake Calhoun trail (trail 31) from Cedar Lake, you will need to be careful when crossing the street at Cedar Lake Avenue and 28th Street because of the railroad tracks and gravel as well as the need to go up a small hill. Since there is no path, you must use the street or sidewalk. Just past Benton Boulevard there is a steep dangerous hill with a stop sign at the bottom. Be very careful! Crossing Dean Parkway at this point, continue south on the boulevard, passing under a bridge where oncoming traffic is a danger. Follow the parkway until you reach the traffic lights at West Lake Street.

To connect to the Lake of the Isles trail (trail 31) from Cedar Lake, cross the railroad tracks and make a left turn onto Benton Boulevard. Follow Benton to where it connects with Dean Parkway and make a left turn onto Dean. Take notice of the well-marked, young-duckling crossing after which you will need to gain a little speed in order to reach the top of the small hill with a three-way stop sign. After crossing and taking a left to head north, you are on the Lake of the Isles trail.

See Minneapolis map, page 91

⚠ Caution   Between Glenwood Avenue and Interstate 394 there is a treacherous combination of a steep, short hill and an adjacent sharp curve. The path crosses some busy roads, particularly State Highway 55. The pavement near the Cedar Lake parking lot is ragged and deformed. It might be better to walk, rather than skate, through this area. The section of the trail near Interstate 394 between Birch Pond and Brownie Lake is used by both skaters and walkers.

34 Minnesota Valley State Trail
A "Fair" Trail

This trail provides a gentle four-mile skate, nearly ten miles when the extension is completed. Take time to visit area shops and maybe the Little 6 Bingo & Casino or the races at Canterbury Downs. Horseback riding is also available in Shakopee.

Where   Shakopee, twenty-five miles southwest of the Twin Cities

Length   4 miles. 5-6 mile extension to be completed by summer 1992.

Difficulty *Beginner*

Surface   Good

Terrain   Trail is mostly flat, following the Minnesota River through wooded areas, past scenic Nyssen's Lake, and by an old brewery.

Facilities Portable restrooms, parking lot

Phone   Nature Center   (612) 492-6400

Get There   Take Interstate 35W south to State Highway 13 and go west toward Shakopee. Continue through Shakopee until one block before the intersection of State Highway 101 and U.S. Highway 169. (We know that sounds dumb, but you will see that it can be done.) Turn right onto Lewis Street and go 1.5 blocks to the beginning of the trail.

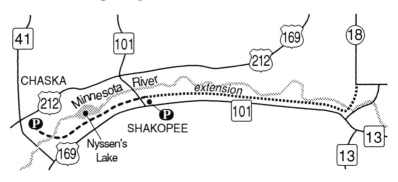

Skate-pooling is hardest on the driver.

35 Normandale Lake
Stopping, Not Shopping, This Dale

This is an excellent path for a modest workout. Each lap is 2.25 miles, lightly used and convenient to those in the southwestern suburbs.

Where	At the junction of Interstate 494 and Normandale Boulevard, in the shadows of the Wang Tower, across the street from Kincaid's, amidst the noise of traffic on 494
Length	2.25 miles
Difficulty	*Intermediate.* A couple of hills and a narrow stretch.
Surface	Good except for a few hundred yards of roughness at the entrance
Terrain	Modestly inclined as the path circles Normandale Lake. Wooded south shore.
Facilities	
Parking	Ample, on west side of Chalet Road across from the lake
Restrooms	At the picnic site
Picnic Site	Near the north parking lot
Other	A walking path with a series of exercise stops
Nearby	Kincaid's is north of the lake across 84th Street. Tony Roma's and Stonewings, an old folks' home for singles, are located at the junction of Normandale Boulevard and 84th. Skating is not allowed on the Bush Lake ski jump.
Phone	Bloomington Parks and Recreation (612) 887-9601
Get There	Take Interstate 494 to Normandale Boulevard, then south to West 84th Street. Proceed west to the intersection where 84th becomes East Bush Lake Road, turn south onto Chalet Road, and go a short distance to the parking lot on your right.

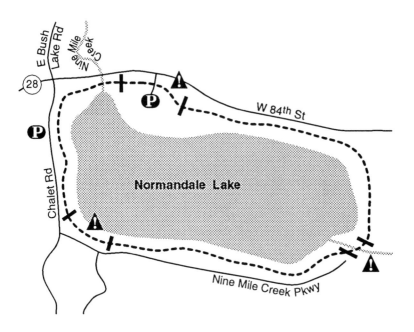

⚠️ **Caution** At the southeastern end of the lake there is a moderately steep incline with a bridge at the bottom. Be careful on the downhill slope of the very narrow (as little as two-feet wide) section that runs alongside busy 84th Street on the northern end of the lake. There is rough pavement along the southwest portion of the trail.

36 North Hennepin Trail Corridor
The Trail That Gives a Dam

This is a simple, well-maintained path that offers a full afternoon's round-trip skate for the whole family. It runs between the Elm Creek Park Reserve and the Coon Rapids Dam.

Where   Maple Grove and Coon Rapids

Length   7.5 miles

Difficulty   *Beginner.* Flat and straight.

Surface   Excellent

Terrain   The trail is well-maintained and flat except for a hill and bridge where it crosses over U.S. Highway 169 about 1.5 miles from the Elm Creek Park Reserve access point. The first 1.5 miles heading east from the Elm Creek access take you through residential areas, after which the scenery changes to a more rural setting of woods and open fields.

Facilities

Parking   At both access points

Restrooms   At both ends of the trail and midway in Oak Grove City Park

Food   There are vending machines at the Coon Rapids access and a concession stand at the Elm Creek Park Reserve access point.

Picnic Sites   At both ends of the trail

Other   The Coon Rapids Dam is adjacent to the Coon Rapids access point. Elm Creek Park Reserve has a playground and swimming about one mile from the parking lot.

Phone   Hennepin County Parks   (612) 559-9000
    Elm Creek Visitor Center   (612) 424-5511

Get There   *Elm Creek Park Reserve (Maple Grove) access.* From Minneapolis, take Interstate 94 west to County Road 81; go north on 81 about six miles to Territorial Road and turn right. The park entrance is one block farther on your right.

Coon Rapids Dam Regional Park (Brooklyn Park) access. From Minneapolis, take Interstate 94 west to State Highway 252 and go north four miles to County Road 30 (93rd Avenue North). Go west on 30 for three-quarters of a mile to Russell Avenue and then north about one mile to the park entrance, which is on the right.

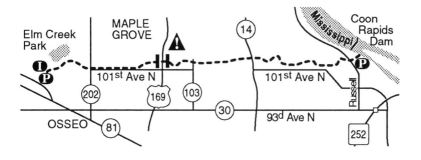

⚠ Caution   Be aware of the hill and bridge located at the crossing of U.S. Highway 169.

37 Opus Loop Trail System
Loop de Loop

This is a peaceful path with many intersecting segments that provide exceptional variety and is especially quiet on weekends due to the reduced office traffic.

Where   Minnetonka, near the Opus Complex alongside U.S. Highway 169 between State Highway 62 and Interstate 494

Length   3.2 miles

Difficulty   *Beginner.* Flat to gently rolling.

Surface   Excellent

Terrain   The trail rambles through a well-landscaped office park containing woods, ponds, town houses, tennis courts, and a pool.

Facilities

Parking   In any of the many office building parking lots

Restrooms   Only at neighboring restaurants

Food   None on the trail. Refreshments at local gas stations and convenience stores.

Other   Exercise stops along the trail

Nearby   Sherlock's Home is a restaurant famous for its authentic hand-pulled English beer and a kitchen that produces genuine English fare. Toros of Aspen has a typical Tex-Mex menu with lime wedges polluting otherwise serviceable beers.

Phone   Minnetonka Loop Trail Corridor (612) 938-7245

Get There   Take the Bren Road exit off U.S. Highway 169 and go west. Keep to the left as you pass the PHP building that is on your right as you enter the Opus Complex. Parking is available in any of the building parking lots. Reconnoitering can be difficult due to the one-way nature of most, but not all, of the local roads.

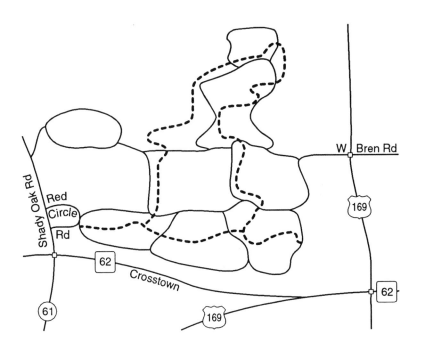

⚠ **Caution** The trail has many intersections with the complex's roadways.

38 Phalen-Keller Regional Park
No Failin' To Enjoy

A scenic and conveniently located trail with plenty of activities for a day's outing. You can connect to the Gateway Segment of the Willard Munger State Trail (trail 21) by crossing Frost Avenue north of this trail.

Where On the border of St. Paul and Maplewood, approximately three miles northeast of downtown St. Paul

Length The combined outer ring is 3.65 miles. The loop around Lake Phalen is 2.9 miles and that circling Round Lake is 1 mile.

Difficulty *Beginner.* Fairly flat.

Surface Good. Portions of the east side have been recently resurfaced. Skating in only one direction. Two thirds of the bike/skate route is shared with walkers, separated by a yellow line.

Terrain Over gently rolling hills, the trail traverses a beautiful wooded area through which a creek connects Lake Phalen and Round Lake. There are several bridge crossings on the west side.

Facilities

Parking The biggest lot is on the southwest side, just off Wheelock Parkway. Other lots are located near the middle west side and north side of Lake Phalen. Ample parking also exists on the north side of Round Lake off Frost Avenue.

Restrooms At the beach house, pavilion, and lakeside activity center on the southwest side of Lake Phalen. Also in Keller Park on the north side of Round Lake.

Picnic Sites Throughout Phalen and Keller parks

Food Snack bars in the beach house, pavilion, and lakeside activity center

Pavilion On southwest side of Lake Phalen, with kitchen facility. Available for large groups by reservation.

Beach House Has changing rooms

Lakeside Activity Center

Canoe, sailboat rentals, fishing pier, and instructional swimming beach. Open shelter is available for group rental.

Golf Two public courses: Phalen, adjacent to the west side of the lake, and Keller, just north of Frost Avenue on the north side of Lake Phalen and Round Lake

Phone

St. Paul Parks and Recreation	(612) 488-7291
Ramsey County Parks	(612) 777-1707
Phalen Beach Concession Stand	(612) 774-9759
Phalen Beach House	(612) 776-9833
Phalen Golf Course	(612) 778-0424
Keller Golf Course	(612) 484-3011

Get There From downtown St. Paul take Interstate 35E about two miles and exit on Wheelock Parkway. Go east 1.5 miles, crossing Arcade Street into the park entrance. Continue on Wheelock about one-quarter of a mile and turn left into the parking lot.

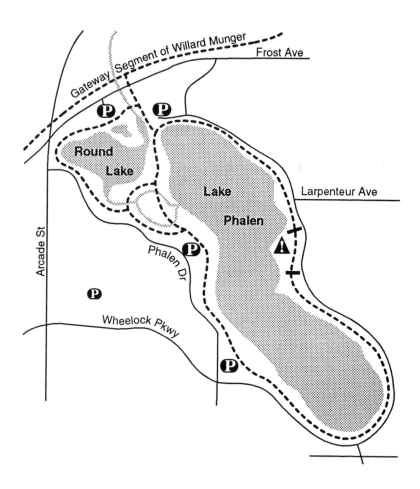

⚠ Caution The middle of the eastern side of the Lake Phalen trail has a gradual uphill slant. Particular care should be exercised on the downhill slant; it is fairly steep and has been the scene of many skating spills. The bridge surfaces are easy to cross but the path is narrow and open to all traffic.

Roll Call

39 Rice Creek West Regional Trail
Crispy

The many busy streets that cross this trail spoil an otherwise scenic and relaxing path. Some may choose to skate just the 1.5 miles between University Avenue and State Highway 65, a stretch suitable for the beginner.

Where   Fridley, eight miles north of Minneapolis

Length   2.5 miles

Difficulty   *Intermediate.* A couple of short, steep hills and many busy intersections.

Surface   Good

Terrain   Flat, open areas on the west end passing a small pond. Midway, the trail follows the creek through a heavily wooded but flat region. The trail passes through a combination of commercial, residential, and park scenery before ending abruptly at the Anoka County line.

Facilities

Parking   The biggest lot is at the west end of the trail and there are others along the way, including two just beyond Columbia Arena in Locke Park that are ideally located if skating only the portion between University Avenue and State Highway 65. There is also a lot at the east end of the trail off 69th Avenue North.

Restrooms   At the park shelter midway through the trail and at the east end of trail

Picnic Sites   Tables are scattered along the trail. In Locke Park there is a shelter with fireplace and running water.

Other   Archery range, horseshoes, soccer field

Phone   Anoka County Parks   (612) 757-3920

Get There   Take University Avenue (State Highway 47) 1.5 miles north of Interstate 694 to the park entrance on your left. At the tee turn right and follow the road into the parking lot.

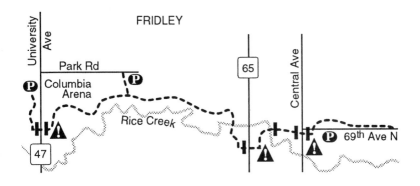

⚠**Caution**   Three busy intersections require attention: University Avenue, State Highway 65, and Central Avenue. The approach to 65 is downhill but the right turn at the bottom is flat. Just beyond the Sunliner Motel there is a steep downhill slope into the woods followed by a steep uphill stretch on the other side of the bridge over the creek.

40 Root River State Trail
A Hoot on the Root

This is one of the most scenic trails in the state. The path runs along the Root River, passing by abundant wildlife including that of the Lost Lake Game Refuge. Excellent choice for a weekend excursion.

Where　　110 miles southeast of the Twin Cities, 30 miles southeast of Rochester, connecting Fountain and Rushford

Length　　28.5 miles

Difficulty　　*Intermediate*. Rolling hills and curves.

Surface　　Good

Terrain　　The trail lies mostly on old railroad bed with a 3°-5° grade over the first two miles leaving Fountain. There is a steep hill located about six miles from Fountain, before the city of Lanesboro. Parts of the trail follow the river, winding through the hardwood forests and meadows of southeast Minnesota. Skating from west to east is a slightly downhill trip. A spectacular and colorful view of the changing leaves is provided in the fall.

Facilities

Parking　　At both ends of the trail and in several towns along the trail

Restrooms　　Portables in Fountain; permanent facilities in Lanesboro, Whalan, and Rushford

Picnic Sites　　Available at all access points

Lodging　　There are at least seven quaint bed and breakfasts along the trail.

Nearby　　Lanesboro offers a variety of activities including summer stock theater, which is comprised of professionals and local talent, and tours of the cheese factory and winery. Andy's Creative Woodery can build whatever you can't find in the Twin Cities' department stores.

The Old Barn Resort located just outside the city of Lanesboro has superb camping and overnight facilities. Tours are available at the Niagara and Mystery caves located southeast of Spring Valley.

You might enjoy the Amish shops and tours in Harmony. Fountain has its famous sink holes for your examination. Rushford provides restaurants and overnight accommodations just thirty feet off the trail.

Phone   Historic Bluff Country Information   (507) 886-2230
Root River Trail Center, Lanesboro   (507) 467-2552
Rochester Trails and
   Waterways Unit, DNR   (507) 285-7176
For additional Bed and Breakfast information
   call 1-800-657-7025 or (507) 467-2525

Get There   *Fountain access on the west end.* From the Twin Cities, take U.S. Highway 52 south through Rochester into the small town of Fountain. Follow County Road 8 east about one mile where parking is available on the south side of the road.

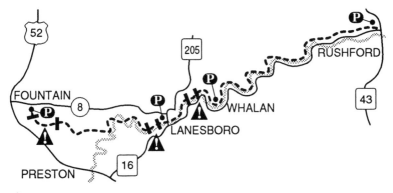

⚠ Caution   Be wary of building up too much speed over the long downhill grade leaving Fountain. The steep hill approaching Lanesboro should be traversed slowly. Between Lanesboro and Whalan, the trail also crosses roads and wooden bridges.

113

41 Sand Creek / Coon Creek Trail
Creaky

This is a good path for local residents but not worth a long drive.

Where	Coon Rapids
Length	4.5 miles
Difficulty	*Beginner*. Flat.
Surface	Good
Terrain	Flat. The trail follows Sand Creek through a tree-lined residential area.

Facilities

Parking	At Lions Coon Creek Park off Hanson Boulevard
Restrooms	At the beginning of the trail
Food	Concession stand in Lions Coon Creek Park
Picnic Site	Covered and uncovered tables with barbecue at the trailhead
Other	At beginning of the trail, playground with softball diamonds and basketball courts. A few scattered benches lie along the way.
Nearby	Hardee's is located two blocks from the Lions Coon Creek Park on Hanson Boulevard. There is a food market with a nifty bakery on Hanson, a block from the park.
Phone	Coon Rapids Parks and Recreation (612) 755-2880
Get There	From downtown Minneapolis, take Interstate 94 west thirteen miles to State Highway 169. Go north on 169 eight miles to State Highway 242 (Main Street), then east about four miles and turn right on Hanson Boulevard. Continue on Hanson for one-half mile and turn left into Lions Coon Creek Park.

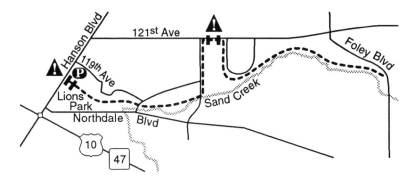

⚠ **Caution** The wooden bridge at the beginning of the trail may be difficult to cross. The path is briefly interrupted near 121st Avenue by railroad tracks. Although the intersecting streets do not carry heavy traffic, be careful crossing them.

42 Shingle Creek Trailway / Palmer Lake
Concreek

Useful for an in-town workout but not very scenic. On its southern end, the trail connects to Memorial Parkway Trail (trail 33) over a rough section about a block long.

Where   Brooklyn Center

Length   Shingle Creek   4.0 miles
                  Palmer Lake   2.9 miles

Difficulty   *Intermediate*. Most of the trail is suitable for a beginner but the bridges over the highways have difficult spiral approaches.

Surface   Good

Terrain   Flat. Uneventful grassland and cement. No view of Palmer Lake from the trail. Shingle Creek Trailway passes through commercial zones except for the Central Park and Garden City Park area.

Facilities

Parking   At East and West Palmer Lake Parks, Nature Area parking lot, and Central Park

Restrooms   Palmer Lake Nature Area (east and west ends) and at Central and Garden City parks. Also midway, off 69th Avenue North.

Palmer Lake Nature Area (east and west ends)

Restrooms, basketball courts, softball diamonds, and play area. Tennis courts at west Palmer Lake only.

Central Park / Garden City Park

Softball diamonds, basketball court, playground, very nice restaurant facilities, exercise stations. Tennis courts in Central Park. Community center with sauna, exercise room, and swimming pool.

Phone   Brooklyn Center Parks
               and Recreation   (612) 569-3400

Get There   From downtown Minneapolis, take Interstate 94 eight miles west to Shingle Creek Parkway. Follow Shingle Creek north for about two miles to 69th Avenue North, turn left, and go one-third mile to West Palmer Lake Park. Turning right at 69th, instead of left, will take you the one-third mile to East Palmer Lake Park.

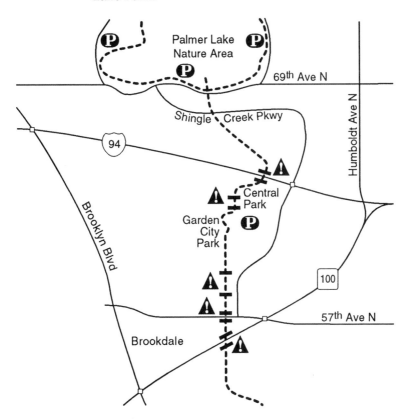

⚠Caution   There is a section about three-quarters of a block long, located just south of Garden City Park that is often underwater during the summer. It can be circumvented by detouring to Shingle Creek Parkway. The freeway overpasses are very difficult to negotiate due to the concrete spiral approaches. Wooden bridges, such as the one in Central Park, require careful crossing.

43 Sibley State Park
Not For Siblings

Most use of this trail comes from nearby residents. Generally not recommended for Twin Citians unless making a camping weekend of the trip. During the summer, bicycle and car traffic can make this trail hazardous.

Where   Approximately 115 miles west of the Twin Cities. Fifteen miles north of Willmar on U.S. Highway 71.

Length   2 miles off-road and 3 miles of on-road bicycle lane

Difficulty *Intermediate.* The on-road section is a narrow, four-foot wide bike lane. The off-road trail crosses County Road 48 (entrance into the park) going downhill. The trail demands control.

Surface   Satisfactory. The fifty-foot section at the junction of County Roads 38 and 48 is particularly rough.

Terrain   Generally flat with the exception of the off-road section that crosses County Road 48 and the fifty-foot uphill portion that is on County Road 38. The rest of the trail has gentle hills and gradual turns. Half of the off-road trail is especially scenic where it follows Lake Andrew.

Facilities

Parking   Ample at both ends of the off-road trail

Restrooms Interpretive Center, Lakeview Campground, and Cedar Hill picnic area

Camping   138 campsites, 52 with electricity. 120-day advanced reservation available for 70 percent of the sites. Others are on a first-come basis.

Picnic Site On edge of Lake Andrew. 140 tables and an open shelter. Recreation field with softball and volleyball.

Other   Boat dock, fishing pier, and swimming area. Boat and canoe rentals available at Cedar Hill picnic area.

Nearby   New London. A quaint town, located four miles east of the park on the Crow River; it has a grocery store, McHale's Family Restaurant, and the Cafe on Main Street.

Cedar Inn Restaurant. Family-style food at the junction of U.S. Highway 71 and County Road 9, just northeast of the park.

Little Melvin's, which is in Spicer on the shore of Green Lake seven miles from the park, is a picturesque restaurant with full bar.

Phone   Sibley State Park Manager
800 Sibley Park Road NE
New London MN 56273
(612) 354-2055

Get There   From Minneapolis, take U.S. Highway 55 west approximately 100 miles to Paynesville. In Paynesville, take a left to go south on State Highway 23 for thirteen miles to New London. Pass through New London's business district to Junction 148, then west (left) onto County Road 148 for three miles. Cross U.S. Highway 71 into the park. The off-road trail starts at the Interpretive Center. Travel time is about two hours.

Sibley State Park

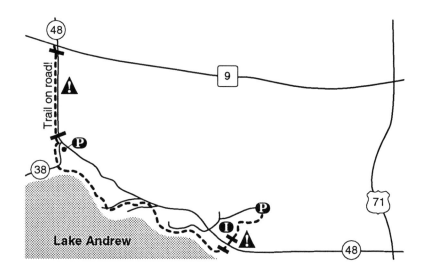

⚠ Caution The downhill section that crosses County Road 48, approximately one-third mile after the start of the trail, warrants a repeated cautionary remark. This decline continues on the other side of the road and is followed by a sharp turn to the right. For the last mile of the County Road 48 on-road trail, the automobile speed limit is 55 MPH.

Jethro is The Man From S.U.I.T. –
Skating **U**rbanely **I**n **T**uxedo.
He decided not to use **H**appily.

44 St. Croix State Park
A Lot to Croix About

There are six scenic miles of good skating here, much of it done by families. You might also explore the many hiking and biking trails located throughout Minnesota's largest state park.

Where   Seventy miles north of the Twin Cities, sixteen miles east of Hinckley

Length   6 miles

Difficulty *Intermediate*

Surface   Good. Smooth with some minor cracking.

Terrain   Flat, except for the area about half a mile from the west end of the trail where there are hills. The rest of the trail is full of curves, winding through the forest and along the St. Croix River.

Facilities

Parking   Ample parking available at both ends of the trail

Restrooms At both ends of the trail

Food   There is a small souvenir shop with limited groceries at the east end of the trail.

Picnic Site At east end of the trail

Other   The park offers great fishing, canoeing, camping, (electrical hookups, primitive and modern group centers), horseback trails, a small grocery store, and a souvenir shop. There is swimming at Lake Clayton Beach and a picnic area with a shelter on the west end of the trail.

Nearby   Hinckley is the nearest town that has a Dairy Queen and municipals (bars, to you city slickers).

New casino (scheduled to open in spring 1992) is located two miles east from Interstate 35 and State Highway 48 exit.

Tobie's serves its famous caramel rolls and beverages. You can also stop and play a round of miniature golf or visit Bohn's Petting Zoo located behind Tobie's.

Phone   St. Croix State Park Manager   (612) 384-6591

Get There Take Interstate 35 north to the State Highway 48
               exit (Tobie's exit). Go east on 48 for sixteen miles to
               the St. Croix State Park entrance. Turn right into
               the park and go five miles to the park headquarters.

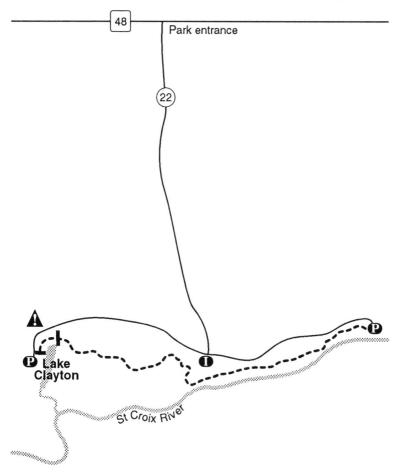

⚠ Caution Beware of the area one-half mile from the west end
               of the trail because of its steepness and curves. This
               portion is clearly marked with caution signs.

45 William O'Brien State Park
St. Croix Cruisin'

This is an excellent path for a modest workout. It is lightly used and located in an extremely attractive and popular part of the state.

Where The trail runs along the edge of William O'Brien State Park, south to Marine on St. Croix.

Length 2 miles

Difficulty *Beginner.* A gently rolling and lightly used trail.

Surface Good, except the portion near Marine on St. Croix – rains often wash mud and stones over the trail.

Terrain The northern section near William O'Brien rolls through open prairie and subsequently tapers downhill through wooded fields to Marine on St. Croix.

Facilities

Parking There is off-street parking near the small commercial district of Copas at the northern end of the trail and very ample parking in William O'Brien State Park. Also street parking in Marine on St. Croix, at the southern end of the trail

Food Crabtree's Kitchen in Copas is a family restaurant with heavy, stick-to-the-ribs home cooking.

At the southern end of the trail in Marine on St. Croix, the Brookside Bar and Grill and the Voyager Cafe are great for lunch or dinner, and the Village Scoop is widely known for its ice cream. The Marine General Store carries everything you need for outside dining.

Nearby Marine on St. Croix is a lovely village with the atmosphere of New England. It provides access to the St. Croix, as well as to the facilities of William O'Brien State Park, including camping, showers, picnic grounds, swimming, fishing, canoe rental, bike trails, firewood, and an interpretive center.

The Trail's End Restaurant and Bar is just north of the trail, near Scandia at the junction of State Highways 95 and 97.

William O'Brien State Park

Phone   William O'Brien State Park   (612) 433-0500

Get There Go east on State Highway 36 to Stillwater, then north on State Highway 95 to parking in Marine on St. Croix.

⚠ Caution The southern portion can be washed out from rains.

Indoor Sites

Indoor rinks provide a safe, controlled, learning environment for both children and adults. The musical accompaniment (many rinks offer Christian, oldies, pop-rock, and other theme nights) adds a special enjoyment to the skating experience. These rinks make an ideal outing for fund-raisers, private parties, and birthdays. In addition to normal open skating, many rinks dedicate special times for adults, pre-school, and family skating, as well as for rollerhockey leagues.

Not all roller skating rinks allow in-line skating. Some rink owners feel that in-line skating is too incompatible in speed and style with traditional roller skating to allow them on the same floor. Additionally, there is concern over gouges to the rink surface due to the exposed metal on some in-line skates or marks of the surface by the skates' brakes. All of the rinks listed here do allow in-line skates, but some of these rinks enforce restrictions on exposed metal bearings and black stoppers. Be sure to call ahead to verify that your skates are acceptable.

Most indoor rinks listed here sell in-line skates but do not rent them. They commonly provide full snack bars and, in some cases, video games, lockers, and semi-private rooms. Open skating admission runs about $3-5 for a session lasting from two to four hours. Call ahead for the schedule.

The Metrodome in downtown Minneapolis is a unique place to skate (during the winter months), if for no other reason than its extensive size – only about 2.5 laps per mile. Skating is allowed on two levels, beginners on the lower, and experienced skaters, including many competitive racers, on the upper. Typical attendance is one thousand or more. Normal hours are 5:00-9:00 P.M. weekdays and noon to 6:00 P.M. weekends, when open. Concessions and a coat check are available.

The following indoor rinks allow in-line skating. It is advisable to call ahead for skating times as well as for information about restrictions that may apply to the use of in-line skates.

Greater Minnesota Area

Brownsdale
The United States Roller Rink
Brownsdale MN 55918
(507) 567-2539

Cambridge
World On Wheels Skate Center
South Highway 65
Cambridge MN 55008
(612) 689-4200

Fargo
Skateland Skate Center
3302 10th Avenue SW
Fargo ND 58103
(701) 235-0555

Faribault
Faribault Family Skating and Banquet Center
112 Northeast 5th Street
Faribault MN 55021
(507) 334-4776

Hibbing
Fairgrounds
Hibbing MN 55746
(218) 263-9860

Lake City
Countryside South Roller Rink and Ballroom
Highway 63 South
Lake City MN 55041
(612) 345-3877

Mankato
Skatin' World
1800 Apache Boulevard
Mankato MN 56001
(507) 625-2507

Monticello
Monticello Roller Rink
Interstate 94 and Highway 25
Monticello MN 55362
(612) 295-3858

Indoor Sites

New Ulm
Izzy-Dorry's Rink
509 20th North
New Ulm MN 56073
(507) 354-6626

Park Rapids
Skateland
300 South Park
Park Rapids MN 56470
(218) 732-4668

Rush City
The Skate Zone
P.O. Box 674
Rush City MN 55069
(612) 358-9996
If no answer, (715) 463-2798

St. Cloud
Skatin' Place
3302 Southway Drive
St. Cloud MN 56301
(612) 252-9768

Superior, Wisconsin
World Of Wheels Skate Center
1218 Oakes Avenue
Superior WI 54880
(715) 392-1031

Willmar
Wheel Fun Skate Center
1300 Southeast Lakeland Drive
Willmar MN 56201
(612) 235-8520

Woodbury
Wooddale Recreation Center
2122 Wooddale Drive
Woodbury MN 55125
(612) 735-6214

Minneapolis Area

Cheep Skate
11100 Cedar Road
Junction of County Roads 73 and 16
Minnetonka MN 55343
(612) 544-3158

Cheep Skate
3075 Coon Rapids Boulevard
Coon Rapids MN 55433
(612) 427-8981

Metrodome
Downtown Minneapolis
Minneapolis MN 55415
(612) 941-1916 (SwitcH*it*® Interchangeable Skate System)

Roller Garden
5622 West Lake Street
(One block west of State Highway 100)
St. Louis Park MN 55416
(612) 929-5518

Saints Bloomington
Family Roller Skating Center
311 West 84th Street
Bloomington MN 55420
(612) 888-9311

Skateland Skate Center
7306 Lakeland Avenue North
Brooklyn Park MN 55428
(612) 425-5858

Skateville
Family Roller Skating Center
201 River Ridge Circle
Burnsville MN 55425
(612) 890-0988

St. Paul Area

Saints North
1818 Gervais Avenue
Maplewood MN 55109
(612) 770-3848

Skatedium Roller Rink
1251 Arundel Avenue
St. Paul MN 55117
(612) 489-7633

General Information Phone Numbers

Department of Natural Resources
Division of Parks and Recreation
Information Center
500 Lafayette Road
St. Paul MN 55155-4040
(612) 296-4776
Within Minnesota: 1-800-652-9747, ask for the DNR
Hearing impaired: (612) 296-5484

Minnesota Office of Tourism
Farm Credit Building
375 Jackson Street
St. Paul MN 55101
(612) 296-5029
1-800-657-3700

International In-line Skating Association (IISA™)
3033 West Lake Street
Suite 300
Minneapolis MN 55416
(612) 924-2348
1-800-FOR-IISA

Please Write to Us

The number of suitable skating paths throughout Minnesota is growing. City, county, and state park systems are continually paving and improving existing trails as well as creating new ones. If you have discovered a favorite trail that is not covered in this book, we would love to hear about it. Please send us a note at:

> The Squarest Wheels
> Wow Publishing
> P.O. Box 16371
> Minneapolis MN 55416

If You Would Like to Order This Book . . .

Let's Skate Minnesota! can be purchased at most popular bookstores, major retailers where skates are sold, and your local bike and sporting goods stores. You may also order directly by sending the number of books desired along with your check or money order, at $9.95 each, made out to Adventure Publications, P.O. Box 269, Cambridge MN 55008. Or, you may order with credit card by calling 1-800-678-7006. Add $2.00 for postage and handling. Minnesota residents, please add 6.5% state sales tax ($0.65 per book).

If your club or organization is planning an event, this book can serve as a great premium gift for participants. For example, sponsors of in-line skate races or charity events might include this guide as part of the registration packet. Please call 1-800-678-7006 or (612) 689-9800.